THE
STRESS MANUAL

Recognize and Resolve
the Processes and Results of Stress
in the Professional Teacher

THE
STRESS MANUAL

**Recognize and Resolve
the Processes and Results of Stress
in the Professional Teacher**

Dean Juniper

PETER FRANCIS PUBLISHERS

© 1991   Dean Juniper

Peter Francis Publishers, The Old School
House, Little Fransham, Dereham. Norfolk
NR19 2JP.

British Library Cataloguing in Publication Data

Juniper, Dean
  The stress manual: recognise and resolve the
  processes and results of stress in the professional
  teacher.
  I. Title
  371.104

ISBN 1-870167-25-2

Printed and bound in Great Britain by Biddles Ltd.,
Guildford and King's Lynn.

CONTENTS

Preface

PREFACE

This book generates active programmes in which teachers can participate, either alone or in a group, to reduce and avoid stress while coping with the physiological, emotional and cognitive symptoms caused by stress.

Readers are encouraged to use constructive personal introspection and adopt the self-management techniques suggested.

Many of the ideas and techniques in this manual stem from the Centre for Stress Management, which is at 156 Westcombe Hill, Blackheath, London and at the University of Reading, London Road, Reading. Both these centres have materials available (see Bibliography, page 150), and can arrange counselling and workshops for stress problems.

Please address queries to Stephen Palmer at the Blackheath address or to Dean Juniper at the University of Reading.

Acknowledgements

Professor Cary Cooper, U.M.I.S.T.; Annie Smeath; The Observer; Open Books; The Stanford University Press; C.B.S. International Publishing; Dr. Richard Suinn; Foulsham Ltd; Gordon Shute, University of Reading. Students on diploma and short courses in guidance and counselling at the School of Education.

Dean Juniper
November 1991

1 STRESS: CAUSES AND EFFECTS

1.1 Introduction

Caught in the turmoil of the modern world with its constant changes and innovation, mankind suffers stress. This is very true of today's teaching profession, buffeted on all sides in the course of the professional day. We all think we know just what stress is, but do we all know what to do about it, or do we really recognize it in ourselves and each other?

Stress is that range of psychological and physical symptoms, thoughts and behaviours, which occur when the human mind is overloaded. The fact that any kind of stress is "bad news" needs to be said to contradict the modern cult of "positive stress". Here a creative virtue is probably being made out of a stubbornly-resistant necessity but the maker of it is unaware of how inefficient it really is. In this book the aim is to create a useful manual on not only recognizing and managing stress but also on working to dispel it altogether.

This chapter starts the process by putting "stress" in context, describing symptoms and offering the individual examples and a number of cameos which can be used as the basis for group discussions.

1.2 Recognizing Stress

Stress is both process and result. It is an old term, first used, in the sense of mental unease, to mean 'grief', by Sir Thomas Browne, a seventeenth century poet. Today, as far as the majority of opinion is concerned, the word means a state of physical and mental tension. There are also various sub-textual meanings attached; for instance, it has a strong, male connotation, with overwork held to be its root: an executive image. Stressed persons are often visualized as hand-clenchers, jaw-jutters and brow-furrowers!

Some stressed people do indeed fit this pattern, but it is very far away indeed from being a complete account of human experience.

Stress has many causes and impacts which differ in time and context. It can be cumulative or indirect, immediate or delayed in its manifestations; contrast the man who walks blithely from a train-wreck but collapses six weeks later from the delayed shock, with the girl who takes her own life as soon as she learns that she has been jilted.

Then compare the choking anxiety of a teacher faced with a class of roughs, with the relative inner calm of that same teacher on a school trip accompanying the same lesson wreckers but this time in a neutral context.

Some people learn to live with their stress, and, having accomplished this trick, learn to love it. Some go even further and sanctify it, claiming they could not do without it; it powers their creativity, tones up their performance.

Psychologists call this sort of rationalizing "secondary gain", and stay unconvinced that the cost/benefit in psychological terms really is positive.

Item Groupings

Most stressed people can be said to show a group or cluster of items, over time, in accordance with their individual vulnerabilities and circumstances. These can be classified under three broad groupings:

Physiological (Circulatory,   Digestive,   Respiratory   etc.
          problems)

Emotional   (Depressive, Anxious, Compulsive etc. problems)

Cognitive   (Attention,   Concentration,   Memory   and
          Creativity problems)

This is not, of course, the whole story, but these groups are
used here as the linchpins of the book. A clear picture of
the implications of the items within stress is afforded when
the checklist shown in Fig 1.1, below and on the following
page, is worked through. This recognition of styles of stress
is one of the foundations of insight and consequent action.

Which statements apply to you?

> I have no recognizable stress-style
>
> I have no recognizable stress-style, yet I believe I am
>   stressed
>
> My stress-style follows a depressive pattern
>
> My stress-style follows an anxiety pattern (phobias,
>   fears, panics etc)
>
> My stress-style follows a compulsive pattern (tics,
>   habits, obsessions)
>
> My stress-style is broadly behavioural (temper
>   outbursts, sulks etc)
>
> My stress-style is broadly cognitive (lapses in
>   concentration, forgetting, mental blocks)

My stress-style reflects circulatory symptoms (migraine etc)

My stress-style reflects skin symptoms (nervous rash, eczema etc.)

My stress-style reflects digestive symptoms (dyspepsia, gastric ulcer etc.)

My stress-style reflects postural symptoms (backache, cramps, fibrositis etc.)

My stress-style reflects vestibular symptoms (giddiness etc)

My stress-style reflects asthenic symptoms (fatigue)

My stress-style reflects respiratory symptoms (asthma etc.)

My stress-style reflects infection proneness (repeated colds etc.)

There is a self-punitive aspect to my stress-style

My stress is linked to predictable job-events

My stress is a composite function of domestic and professional pressures

My stress might be eased by job-enrichment

My stress might be eased by intelligent, supportive management

I could help my own stress significantly by a range of self-management techniques

Fig. 1.1 Stress and Stress-Style

The diagram shown below introduces the early stages in the task of understanding the problems of stress (Fig. 1.2). Here the diagram is incomplete (only its inner core is shown) but as we work through the chapter our understanding will grow until the Circle is completed on page 24.

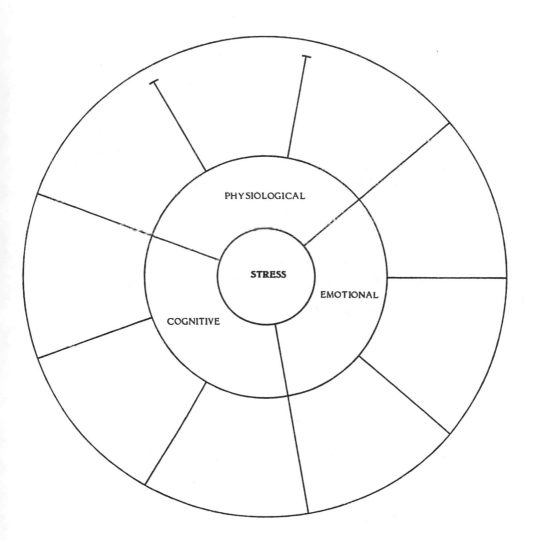

Fig. 1.2   The Stress Disc

When it is complete, it will show comprehensively the three domains of stress, the various symptom patterns lying within those domains, and, in the outer segments, with the cameo characters, the widest range of appropriate remedies, therapies and restorative techniques which can be used individually (self management) and in groups (workshops).

All diagrams have their limitations; this is more limited than most. If the sections were movable, they could be slipped into overlap positions, thereby showing more realistically the realities of individual stress experience. The diagram is also not three-dimensional. Were it thus designed, it might more clearly show time as a factor in stress; how one symptom may replace another, or how stress may accumulate over a period.

A word of caution! All the inner sectors of the diagram, then, are stress-involved and show up in symptom form according to the particular stress-style of the sufferer. Although they appear in separate blocks, they can, in practice, overlap. In terms of personal experience, stress-styles can change over time.

A pattern of unrelieved anxiety, with tension and panic features, which dominates a sufferer's twenties or thirties, can transform itself into a quiet, gnawing depression in the sufferer's forties and fifties.

1.3 Causes of Teacher Stress

If there has been one benefit from the current focus upon the problems of teaching, it has been to force attention on the truth that teachers have always been uniquely stressed. Their recent projection, however, into the wild and unpredictable world of post-modern education, their assignment to cover ground which properly belongs to social work, the vague moral climate in which they are expected to work, the loading on to them of arbitrary theories of management, incentives and learning, the vital and immediate demands made upon them, have all combined to emphasize the instinctual paradoxes and special cognitive demands of their role, bringing their stress into sharp focus.

In terms of its range of potential stress-determinants, teaching appears unique. The role demands:

*   A work-contact milieu with an extending age-gap between teacher and taught

*   In subjects such as Science and Music, an exceptional mix of technical/manipulative with didactic/communicative skills

*   The necessity, whether conscious or otherwise, to maintain disciplinary control

*   A personal openness, rendering the teacher vulnerable to the influence of extra-mural, emotional conflicts and pressures

*   A diurnal work-rhythm based on traditional unresearched term models

*   An annual work-rhythm based on traditional unresearched term models

*   A post-school/college preparation commitment

*   An unregulated exposure to a range of infectious illnesses

*   An imposed appraisal framework with several dimensions, personal, objective etc.

*   An acceptance of political cross-currents and consequences, interrupting relationships with pupils/students

*   A broadly spread and simultaneously detailed attention to tasks within the work-contact milieu, with little opportunity to focus, as a self-protection.

Out of the list those of primary importance can be identified as:

1. Instinctual Challenge

This is, for example, that inevitable summoning up of urges to fight, fly or rest doggo, which every individual, exerting dominance over a group, must feel. The verb "feel" is advisedly used. Experienced teachers performing (another significant word) do not "feel" such urges. But, just the same, they are there, a ground-swell on which an emotional storm can be raised. And the sea is not quiet, because the social weather is becoming rougher and the little classroom pools reflect this change.

2. Performance Vulnerability

It is that special, exclusive anxiety, the sense of being on stage, without the cultural supports given to actors, and under the scrutiny of those seeking reassuring signs of weakness, hesitation, indecision or confusion.

3. Cognitive Dissonances of Complex Kinds

Amongst these is the special demand on certain teachers (Science, Crafts and Music) for a high level mix of technical/artistic/manipulative with didactive/communicative skills. (There is no other profession where performance and teaching must combine so effectively.) Dissonance also occurs in the complicated mismatch inevitably accompanying compartmentalized time-tabling which has to accommodate both learning and teaching styles (an individual teacher's style with multi-learning pupil styles). Then too, the developing mind works to a different routine from the mature intellect, and yet they must mesh in the classroom and hit performance-effective peaks together.

There is also an important, purer cognitive dissonance factor, namely the treadmill effect. Teachers are caught up in a grinding learning machine. The role does not surmount the enormous responsibility of air-traffic controllers; it cannot allow the freedom for reverie that process-workers enjoy. However, there is an inexorability about it. Although it is true that colleagues and pupils offer personal variety, and that syllabus work is still not quite mechanically bolted down, teachers report a feeling of being trapped in an inevitable, imprisoning system.

1.4 Stress-making Situations

On a day-to-day, hour-to-hour basis, we can illustrate through imaginary diary jottings some of these stress-making problems which will appear very familiar to many a teacher today:

> I hardly got the nose of the car out of the gate when that fourth-year girl who is a permanent absentee, started yelling obscenities at me.

> There is an incessant noise coming from the next classroom.

> Two boys in my slowest French set are always trying to sabotage the language laboratory electrics.

> I had to pull a Pakistani and a Jamaican girl apart at lunch-time, otherwise there would have been murder.

> The headmaster sent home (coloured hair) two of my slowest readers five mornings running.

> The overhead projector has broken down again.

There was another break-in last weekend and the police are finger-printing.

I now find I have left all my notes in my car on the other site.

I was well into Religious Knowledge this afternoon when Barbara ... burst into uncontrollable weeping. It seems her father died during the weekend. Why am I told nothing?

What is happening in heavy craft? Three mornings running I have had latecomers returning from being patched up.

I don't know who is responsible for the checking of textbooks, but when I began third year English this morning no less than ten anthologies were pages short.

After that work experience week my programme is in tatters.

Some of these entries may on the surface appear full of humour, but there is an undertow of stress as evidenced by the chart on page 11, Fig. 1.3, adapted from *The Observer's* chart of *Dissatisfaction and Stress Symptoms*.

It is worth noticing that according to the chart Teacher smokers number twice the professional average; one in five is drinking as an emotional release; one in five is taking a prescription drug; four out of ten are actively seeking an exit from the profession.

DISSATISFACTION

STRESS SYMPTOMS

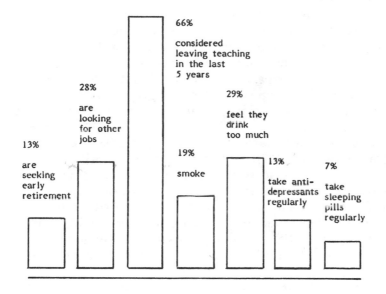

66%

considered
leaving teaching
in the last
5 years

28%

are
looking
for other
jobs

29%

feel they
drink
too much

13%

are
seeking
early
retirement

19%

smoke

13%

take anti-
depressants
regularly

7%

take
sleeping
pills
regularly

Fig. 1.3 Current Teacher Situation

1.5 Cameos

To illustrate the idea of stress there follow several fictional case histories, cameos. These will, of course, be category statements in themselves. It is assumed that the subjects of these cameos describe accurately their symptoms, that they possess some measure of introspective ability and that there is a dynamic relationship between their stressful circumstances and their symptoms.

How may they be used? It is not likely that a reader will find a precise circumstantial fit in any of these cameos. But ground-rules exist to enable approximate matchings to be made. In one, for instance, the stress symptom is a vague dyspepsia, but it might well be migraine and so on. Nor does a single symptom have to reign supreme.

Do not accept these cameos as descriptions of fixed states; they may well be in the process of evolution. The vague dyspepsia, allowed to run on, may convert suddenly into a flaring anxiety in which the tension-focus may move away from the abdomen and express itself in regular panic attacks. Depressed or burned-out Peter (Cameo 3) is still directing the bulk of his anger at external objects, for example, the government. Panic-episodes, seemingly triggered off by the special classroom tensions, characterize another cameo.

The cameos illuminate the inner sectors of the master-diagram (see Fig. 1.2). But they are essentially passive. The subjects do not actively challenge either their stress-provoking circumstances or the symptoms or behaviours which stem from them. In later chapters the initial themes of the cameos will be expanded to bring successive insights to the predicaments of the characters, as the materials accumulate, so that they may be used as focal points for discussions.

The cameos are multi-purpose. They enable

a) a swift overview of the teacher-stress problem via several possible personal identifications, or a recognition of salient features in another sufferer;

b) the hitching of several scenarios to consequent problem-easing processes described in later detail;

c) the stimulation of reader-attention towards the theoretical underpinnings of stress-reduction methods;

d) the encouragement of imagination in the creative handling of personal challenges;

e) the establishing of gender and age impartiality in the characterization of the cameos.

* * * * * * * * *

Cameos 1 and 2 (physiological)

1. Mark

Mark was suffering from monosymptomatic tension dyspepsia, according to the doctor, who, noting Mark was a teacher, had done him the honour of giving him a textbook diagnosis, rather than some folk-medical label. This was about the sum total of his therapeutic effectiveness, as it turned out, since Mark was still monosymptomatically tension dyspeptic six months into the treatment.

'Onset is significant', the doctor had remarked. Onset had been after Mark had gobbled a sandwich while driving up the M6 for the start of term. This had clearly been something of a trigger waiting to be pulled, since within minutes he had experienced a most disturbing indigestion, manifesting itself as extreme tightness in the abdomen, and a fearsome belching.

'I've very little actual pain; do you think it's an ulcer?' Mark asked after about four weeks of dieting, antacids and sedatives. A barium routine showed negative but failed to reassure Mark.

'I'm a phantom two ulcer man on a three ulcer job,' he complained.

'You're a young man of twenty six, trying to cope with an exceptionally demanding job,' the doctor said. 'There's nothing very rare about your condition; in fact it's quite common amongst young people.'

'I'm not **so** young,' Mark said defensively. 'But you're right about the stress. They've lumbered me with the role of "split-site communication co-ordinator". There's a mile between the two sites. When it's not bunking, it's bonking or bashing each other's faces in, and I don't just mean the boys and girls. It's double this and double that, and double-quick if the timetable's to be kept to. It's a good thing I'm a P.E. specialist. I feel on top of the job, but whether I am in fact is another matter. I think it's a family thing, this stomach business. My mother has had a gastric ulcer, and my grandfather perforated his, cranking up a car, so they say.'

2. Gerald

Gerald's eczema developed into a full-blown problem, shortly after the merger and the consequent confusion in the Science Department. He'd always suffered manageable, minimal eruptions on his wrists; in fact since early childhood. But these small patches had been kept in check, seemingly by ointments.

Six weeks into the merger term and after a couple of very upsetting timetabling incidents, the eczema snapped its chain. It covered the backs of both hands and lower forearm with a weeping pustular crust, itching like a hundred fleabites. Gerald had to don gloves and coat his skin with weird, freezing jellies. He had to swallow a range of pills which made him feel as if in Disneyland much of the day. All seemed to have an effect on the eczema for, a week after the end of term, it had shrunk down to a few red patches.

'Thank the Lord, or the Devil Science for that', Gerald said. 'I was more than a mite tired of it all.'

But, the following term, with its attendant confusion, had scarcely begun, when the eczema came back with a bang.

'Do you know what I think?' said Gerald's GP. 'I think this condition is psychosomatic. You've clearly gone above your usual stress threshold.'

Cameos 3, 4 and 5 (Emotional)

3. Peter

Peter waxed quite indignant when the deputy head suggested he might be "burned out".

'I'm not bloody well burned-out', he said. 'That's a fancy American term for bored professionals. I'm not bored, I'm depressed, and for pretty good reasons too.' The deputy head fluttered off, sympathizing, unconvincingly. 'Pity he went', said Peter, 'because I was going on to tell him why; as if he cared. He's part of the problem.'

Peter's staffroom audience now began to excuse itself and sidle out. But Peter had hit his stride and was not to be deterred by fewer and fewer listeners.

'I was going to ask him to put himself in my position,' he went on. 'Fifty one, married and still a sizeable chunk of the mortgage to pay off. I was going to ask him if he relished our having to go cap-in-hand begging for a salary rise to match the cost of living index; not that the COLI ever matched anything real in the way of costs. And whether he'd envisaged himself at fifty one with the honorific and hardly exalted role of Head of Year! And being consistently passed over for promotion!'

'Does he wake every morning with a feeling of despair?' he demanded.

'Does he reflect then that there's precious little chance of amounting to much? Is he sitting on the memory of a couple of text books written, but having them rejected by at least a dozen educational publishers, to say nothing of a novel? Has he ever had the experience of a third year lad saying, politely, "You're out of touch, Sir", when only fifteen years back he was described on a reference as a "little green behind the ears." No, of course not. That's why he's a member of the management echelon at the age of thirty five.'

'I'm not surprised that a man with your capacity for bitter eloquence is dissatisfied', said Eric, one of Peter's younger and thoughtful colleagues.

'Yes, well I am supposed to be an English expert,' said Peter. 'There's a whacking gap between my ambition and my realization. You'll recall that Nietzsche said that, unless you carry chaos within you, you'll never give birth to a dancing star. I've got the chaos right enough, but where's the dancing star?'

'What do you expect from teaching?' Eric asked him.

'I can't recall what I expected,' Peter said. 'Just as I couldn't describe in this half-baked and melancholy state exactly where the interest went. Results, conceivably, but the results are impossible to assess. Feedback, but all one gets is blow-backs.'

'I know the cure for you,' said Eric brightly, 'a change of job.'

'Pray, do me a favour,' Peter said. 'Who do you think is going to employ a man whose only skill is stopping kids moving their lips while they read?'

4. Adele

It was some weeks before Adele actually realized that she had a tension-state, and that it differed in many subtle ways from any ailment she had experienced before.

The first sign was a marked jump in her smoking rate. She went from a steady five a day, carefully and easily slotted into lunch and coffee breaks, to twenty five, which put her virtually onto the tobacco production-line; chain-smoking in the staffroom and even smoking the odd one in the toilet.

Then she had a strange headache almost continuously. It was not like a migraine or a hangover. In fact, she could not be quite sure if it were located in her head. At times it might have been in her stomach or even at the tips of her fingers. Some very strange feelings accompanied it.

There was a vague feeling of unease. When she awoke, it was very faint, but as the day wore on, it became stronger and by evening had often reached the level of alarm. Occasionally, almost always in the afternoon, invariably when she was up to her eyes in fourth year physics, she would experience a panic. She would have the urge to run out of the science wing. The thought in her mind would usually be 'I'm going mad'. How she stood there instructing her class was a miracle.

She described these panics to herself as the 'worst thing in the world'. The process was a rising, rising tension, reaching an unendurable peak, and holding at this level for at least a minute (it felt like an hour) before it fell away. Paradoxically, within ten minutes, the panic might never have occurred; all it left behind was a slight vibration as if one had been severely shaken. And that was all, until the next.

Then there was the weird sensation of being alien, not herself at all. Other times it would seem as if it were a long time ago, perhaps her childhood.

Then there were the daydreams. From time to time it would be similar to being on "automatic pilot", her lips moving, words coming forth, but she would be far away.

Sleeping was also plagued by night-starts. She would wake up after an hour or so, crying out.

'Oh, I wish I did know what was worrying me', she said to herself, 'because if I could tie it down, it might be

possible to target a remedy onto it. I'm supposed to be
a scientist; what I need is something concrete to work
on.'

5. Gillian

Gillian had always been a stickler for discipline and
never considered herself at all unusual in this respect.
One day, however, she heard her art lessons described
sotto voce by one third year to another as 'like a session
on Death Row', and this prompted her to look at herself
afresh. What she saw was a driven woman, both
mercilessly compelling of others, and self-compelled. Her
conspectus showed several areas where she seemed
controlled by inner demands or routines. Most noticeable
were the obsessions. She was forever treble-checking
things, whether she'd locked the flat etc. Then there
were the tunes or phrases, fragments which ran round in
her head, or semi-meaningless jingles.

The worst obsession had a racial basis. She had become
terrified of making inadvertent, racist remarks. A good
quarter of the school was coloured, which meant that the
threat, as she interpreted it, was ever-present. Suppose
she should blurt out some phrase, such as, 'working like
a black?' What if she were to over-criticize some
sensitive, coloured artist's collage? The problem was so
acute that she feared even to glance at a coloured
child's work.

Gillian did not smoke but her drinking was now greatly
increased. A couple of glasses of whisky were required
to put her to sleep, two shorts, at least, on every
occasion she could escape at lunch time, was the rule,
and a half bottle of wine with her supper had become an
unbreakable convention.

Above and beyond everything was the increasing rigidity
in her professional behaviour. She was forever winding up
colleagues and pupils. Everything had to be done to the
book, and preferably yesterday!

Gillian had some insight into the mind's defensive mechanisms, and she understood that obsession often covered for anxiety, indeed could be regarded as a kind of temporary solution to it. She had a vague awareness in her own conscious past of keeping fear away by refusing to face it - by moving a ritual, convention, or habit into its place.

Cameos 6 and 7 (Cognitive)

6. Frank

Frank, who was not given to self-pity or bouts of self-diminishment, had the feeling that the fires had died inside him. He'd always been the ideas-man; ever since his collegiate days they'd looked to Frank for creativity; perhaps mingled with a streak of eccentricity, but none the less a welcome input. Now they'd learned not to expect much, if anything.

The impairment was almost total, covering every aspect of existence. Frank was the only teacher-member of the local Lions. The rest of the club were business men. It was Frank who put the winter programme together. That had been a tradition, but no longer. This year Frank was idea-less, nothing firing inside at all. The Chairman had to step in, and a pig's ear he made of it.

Frank had been a brilliant conversationalist, in an era when such talents were undervalued. Now, he was scared to open his mouth. The words of Socrates came to him. "Man is silent, because he has nothing to say".

'That Socrates was about right,' Frank said to himself. 'I've nothing to say, beyond an anxious query as to whether I'm boring my listener. I'm empty.' As to his teaching, that had become as routine as a waterwheel, and a good deal less useful. A history specialist, our

Frank, at an epoch of ferment and controversy in the subject, when an inventive teacher might have been expected to shine! But Frank's offerings were about as valuable as woodworm in a cripple's crutch.

'I know my judgement and discrimination are as good as ever', said Frank to himself, 'and that being so, all I need to establish myself as a creative person is a flow of ideas. But there's no flow. Yet there needs to be both flow and selective judgement, if I'm to finely inform those young minds.'

7. Jack

Jack at 45 was beginning to wonder if he was suffering from senile dementia. First of, there was the name forgetting. Everybody forgets names, but Jack had developed virtual name-amnesia. He could not recall more than three members of his class. Before he phoned, he had to write names down. Introducing people was a nightmare. Then there was the problem of fluency. If one is a French and German specialist, keeping the words moving is vital. But Jack was failing in that department also.

Holding the thread of an argument was another problem. His span of immediate recall had shrunk so small that he could not recall the start of any chain of reasoning after a moment or so of cut and thrust.

What were even more serious were the confusions in direction or action. He twice drove off through a red light when the pedestrian sign flashed on. Fortunately, there was no traversing traffic. He was also lucky when intending a left turn on a dual carriageway he drove out into the central reservation and then turned left! A lightening U-turn just saved him.

This did not exhaust the laterality problems either. Jack, an enthusiastic squash player, found himself knocking up on the court with his left hand, after a lifetime's practice and play with his right!

At a deeper level of awareness though, Jack knew that emotional conflicts lay behind this mental confusion, not the least because when the result of the brain scan came through, it was full of cautious phrases like 'A very minimal and largely inferential amount of brain damage.'

'Seems to me that the all-knowing really know very little, but hedge themselves around with a few speculative hypotheses,' Jack said to himself. 'My guess is that they can't see anything but feel they must write something. Emotionally blocked and confused, that's what I am. Not emotionally disturbed; I don't feel emotional at all. But worry has got into my higher centres. I've got to use my head to get it out of my head.'

* * * * * * * * * *

1.6 Commentary

All occupations make physical impacts on those who are employed in them. Some of these effects are specialized; others are common to a wide range of occupations. Some are severe, some mild. Long and short-term differences are observable. The impact can be direct or indirect, mono or multi-causal. Here is a list that illustrates a typical, teacher range, working from the least to the most severe:

Fatigue states.

> Common at many ages and stages. Typically severe in first post. Can be seasonally end term-phase linked, with peaks of vulnerability, for example, mid-winter end of term etc. Can be linked to stressful episodes, probably unique to teaching being attributable to the

presentational and disciplinary demands of role.

Vulnerability to Common Infections.

Generally most common for younger teachers with as yet little resistance to pupil-passed infections, colds etc. In few other jobs does essential continuity broken by teacher absence add stress to any relatively inexperienced staff.

Various Allergies, Skin Diseases and Migrainous States.

Many multi-caused, but significant causal elements (school dusts, detergents, anxieties) within the educational environment to trigger and sustain them. Again, because of the presentational and disciplinary, to say nothing of the visual and dexterity demands of teaching, such complaints can generate stress-on-stress.

Postural and Arthritic Conditions.

Diseases of mature teachers, not unique to them. However, presentational nature of teaching make postural demands, together with emotional stress additive, generating high incidence of such complaints among teachers, "disc failures" and crippling sciatic attacks etc. not uncommon amongst the profession.

Circulatory and Digestive Ailments

No commoner in teaching than elsewhere, but little doubt that professional stress can trigger, sustain or exacerbate these. Often indirectly traced both to teaching stress and knock-on effects of drinking, smoking etc. as compensations for such stress. High blood-pressure component of such complaints has been shown to fluctuate with repressed anger or frustration; bio-rhythms of teaching associated with pressure gradients.

1.7 Summary

What theoretical framework encloses these cameos? A general theory of stress must pack together a considerable span of possible causes and probable effects. There is such a mass of potential items involved that only the simplest ordering will suffice at the start.

One such simple arrangement is Balance/Imbalance theory, which attempts to account for stress by viewing it as the variable and diverse product of a negative balance between pressures perceived by a person and the accumulated resources that a person has for standing such pressures.

A negative balance existing and stress emerging mean that pressures exceed defensive capabilities. It allows us to subject our experience to the analysis of an unstable equation, to attempt to fix the emergence of a mood or symptom to those periods when external pressures exceed one's capacity to cope. It directs us to assess our coping strengths. It also focusses our attention upon external pressures. If we wish to chart these processes we can keep a diary of feelings and events because the "self" does exert control over what it sees, thinks and remembers.

Any theory of teacher stress worth its salt must be multi-causal and highly interactive if it seeks to cope with the demands of active stress reducing. It must try to integrate group dynamics, social pressures, instinctual challenge and response, ageing etc. etc. in a simple, practical way. In the following chapters the idea of a self management guide to coping with or even avoiding stress will be discussed and self management practices suggested using the cameo characters as examples.

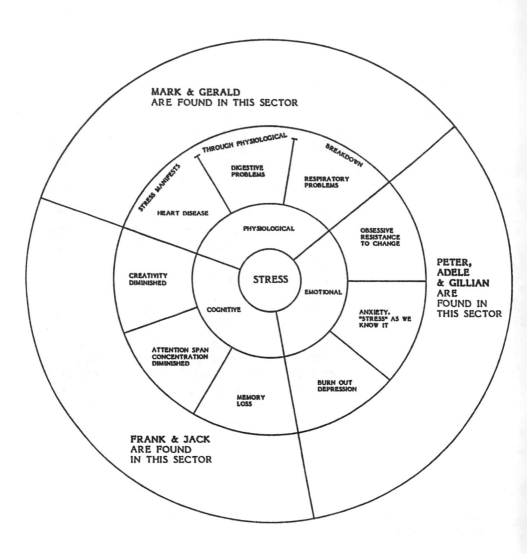

Fig. 1.4 The Stress Disc Completed

2 OVERCOMING DEPRESSION

2.1 Introduction

Whenever a fresh strategy, that is, an action, is introduced to combat a problem, no matter what form it takes, almost everyone adopting this strategy seems to improve to some extent in the short term. This is equally true for both physical and psychological remedies.

Little is known about the reason for such improvements, although auto-suggestion probably plays an important role. Thus a group approach to strategies could prolong an improvement phase, particularly because auto-suggestion often plays a large part in group participation.

This book is a self management guide and, although it can be easily adapted for group purposes, one must bear in mind that such a scheme is very much dependent upon experimental learning, personal shaping and the wealth of accumulating the insights that self-discovery can bring. Also any list of strategies applicable to the relief of teacher stress must of necessity be carefully arranged in order to avoid becoming unwieldy and difficult to use. The message emerging for relief of teacher stress is the necessity for constructive, personal introspection, because a sufferer's own analysis and memories of previous attempts to improve can help in this.

Various rules must be made and followed, otherwise strategies adopted will become unwieldy to select and make use of. Therefore foundation items, techniques useful in their own right which can be joined with others later, must be adopted first; emotional problems must not be divided up, but rather tied together by therapeutic threads; sufficient theory must back each technique; and finally each therapy must be matched to the problem.

These rules should be followed with care so that teachers achieve a balance and do not overreach themselves.

2.2 Categories

To achieve this balance it is advisable to work through categories, however rough they may be; the themes of the cameos can be used to illustrate these.

In this chapter the first category, Depression, will be considered and illustrated by Peter's problem in cameo 3. (Other issues which are implied in his cameo, such as values or interests, will come up in the workshop sections in later chapters). Ways of dealing with and overcoming depression will be discussed and these can also be applied to the workshops shown later in the book. In subsequent chapters other categories will be dealt with, such as Anxiety (Adele's Cameo), Compulsion (Gillian's Cameo), etc.

Just as in Mathematics, no matter how complex the problem is, there are only four basic actions to take, so in self management therapies we also have to have a limited framework of action.

They consist in this case of what can be called nine strategies through which the self manager or indeed groups can work. These are described on the page 27, in section 2.3.

2.3 Strategies to Eliminate Symptoms

A symptom can take the form of an idea, an action (willed or compelled), a feeling (describable or indescribable), or a reflex. In self managed therapy there is a limited framework of nine strategies which can be used in the elimination of a symptom. A symptom can be

1) relabelled, usually to minimize its significance and thus isolate it;

2) ignored, (for example, crowd it out by other thoughts, and thus diminish it)

3) extinguished

4) encouraged, (and thus exhausted)

5) recorded, (and thus, paradoxically, diminished in frequency)

6) conditioned to its disadvantage (for example, compelled to associate with powerful opposite ideas, actions or feelings, and so, squeezed)

7) confronted (and broken by an act of self-will)

8) substituted for (intentionally or accidentally by a more or less painful idea, action or feeling)

9) eliminated (by a powerful tranquilliser).

2.4 Analysis

The would-be self manager should ask him or herself the following questions:

When?

Has everything to do with time?

Does the problem vary with time?

Is it phasic?

Is it worse or better or absent at specific times of the day etc?

Is it tied to some internal mechanism, or does it respond to something outside?

Why?

Why does the problem arise?

Is the answer clear?

Does there appear to be more than one answer?

Is an answer necessary?

To whom might one go to seek an answer?

Which?

Is the problem one of many?

Is it the most important problem?

How?

How does the problem manifest itself?
     By feeling?
     Of choices?
     By someone's behaviour?
     Not being able to identify the problem?

Who?

Who are the persons involved?

Where?

Does the problem occur everywhere?

Is it linked with places?

Armed with these questions and using Peter's cameo as reference we can discuss the various methods of tackling depressive states, often a cause of stress.

2.5 Depression

As we know depressive thoughts can produce feelings of depression. Thus it is important to identify some of the areas where these thoughts can operate.

Low self-regard
This is an unrealistic downgrading of self in areas which are particularly important, for example, career, appearance. Often the person will draw unfavourable comparisons with others in his own group, rating himself inferior.

Ideas of deprivation/self-pity
'Nobody likes me' etc.
These thoughts can occur however great the evidence to the contrary.

Self-criticism and self-blame
'It is my fault' 'I am to blame'.

Overwhelming problems and duties
Problems and responsibilities considered minor are magnified when one is in a depressed state and duties etc. crowd in.

Self-commands

'I must do this'. 'It is my duty to make sure this happens'. There are constant self-instructions, nagging to do impossible or impractical things.

Escapist and suicidal wishes

There is a wish to withdraw from unsolvable problems. Day-dreaming of "far away places" or imagining oneself in an entirely different situation is a form of escapism. In very severe cases there is the notion of suicide as being the only escape.

Inappropriate personal myths

Some depressives have personal myths, often causing them suffering when they clash with circumstances. For example, do you visualize yourself as a Hero, dramatically beset by difficulties yet holding your own; or, do you visualize yourself as a Saviour, not so much a miracle worker, but a steady solver of problems and upholder of the weaker brethren?

None of these myths is necessarily irrational when placed in the appropriate context and used with restraint. There are situations in which heroes are necessary and society applauds their successful role-taking. Problems arise when confusions between different roles take place. For example, a persistent Hero is snubbed by a lack of crisis. Peter, the subject of Cameo 1 (Depression), is a good example of a rejected Saviour, consumed by bitterness.

2.6   Countering Depressive Thoughts through Self Management

When an individual is depressed, he can learn to counteract his automatic reactions to events by testing them objectively and getting them in perspective. When he is not depressed, a similar analysis of irrational thoughts can reduce his vulnerability to future depression. First, however, he must recognize his own sensitivities, exaggerated or inappropriate reactions and the cause-effect relationship between external events and internal discomfort. Next he must recognize and evaluate the thoughts which are specific to low moods and then alter the misconceptions, superstitions and false philosophies that lead to such feelings.

It is vital to possess a knowledge of those circumstances which trigger depression. Therefore a sensitivity list is valuable for analysing depressive feelings. For example:

1.   What is this depressive feeling?
2.   What was happening when I first felt this?
3.   Is this an area in which I am particularly sensitive?
4.   Have I thought in this precise way before?
5.   Are the circumstances the same as the previous occasion?

Having identified the thought preceding the feeling, try to classify it in one of the group mentioned in 2.5, for example, low self-regard, self-pity etc.

In his book *Depression* (1972), Beck introduces the term "automatic thoughts". These thoughts are items that push one into feelings of despair. They are usually of the 'I'm no good' type. Such thoughts seem to be highly-condensed representations of more elaborate ideas, rather like short-hand, so that a complicated thought occurs within a split second. If a person can identify such thoughts, see them in perspective, and correct them, he can neutralize some of their effects. Here two points need emphasizing:

1. An individual is normally aware only of the following sequence of events:

EVENT (stimulus) ....EFFECT (depression)

2. But, in actual fact, the sequence is:

EVENT ....THOUGHT ....EFFECT

Thus, if there can be rationalization or explanation of the thought, the effect could well be changed.

These thoughts can also influence other aspects of depression, for example, loss of drive. If, for instance you were to say 'I won't be able to do it', your drive to do it is sapped. You have to stand back and distance yourself from these thoughts.

2.7 Strategies to Combat Depression.

There are wider implications to a state of depression than the individual thinking that goes with it, since depression is a little orchestration of emotion and events. However, once thoughts have been identified and classified and a way of conquering them has been found, it is useful to have a checklist for discovering what inaccurate assessments have been going on in one's mind.

A comprehensive strategy is required to exert leverage to lift a depression. By surveying a depression from the vantage point of one day at a time, ten possible leverage systems can be found and a checklist made.

A copy of this checklist for your own use is shown in Figure 2.2 on page 37. Its purpose is to provide a day-to-day record of progress made towards lifting the depression as the list is completed. The idea is that the checklist should be completed once a day, and treated as a guideline for each problem met. Using the character, Peter, from Cameo 1 in chapter 1, as a guide for our checklist, we can follow the progress of his attempt at the self management of his depression. Figure 2.1 on page 33 shows a completed "Tactics for One Day Checklist".

Note the following important points:

He is being thoroughly honest with himself but at the same time not over-burdening himself with detail. When a single approach seems appropriate, he tries it.

STAGE OR ACTION	INTENSITY/DESCRIPT.	DESCRIPTION OF ACTION/PLAN
1. Morning Awakening	C. Very gloomy	Went for a 10 min. jog & did a fresh isometric routine
2. Routine Depressants	B. Usual nonsense; no parking place. Overnight parkers?	Will walk/cycle to school unless weather is impossible. Only 2 miles.
3. Stimuli situations	B. Burst of depressive thoughts midmorning	Burst occurred as we discussed poet, Chatterton. Tried thought stopping technique with success
4. Other persons	B. I talked gloomily in staff room	Certain now I'm using Philip as resonator for the depression; will make sure I meet him where we can't talk intimately.
5. Feeding oneself	B. could hardly face breakfast despite jog.	See no. 7 for Action, provided an idea for Activity-Scheduling
6. Upswings	A. Good upswing just before lunch!	Also see no. 7
7. Anticipation		From 5: slipped out at lunch time & bought some cheap! smoked salmon for our supper. Booked theatre trip with wife, as per schedule, ten days on.
8. Reinforcements		Reinforced upswing by sending research scripts to English Adviser; from whom a quid pro quo will be expected daily.
9. Using an unconscious mind		Played through "mother going on" cassette & practised "switch off" technique.
10. Presleeping & Sleeping	B. Felt a little tense as I went to bed.	Have persuaded wife to fit sound-deadening curtains to bedroom.

Fig. 2.1 Tactics Checklist Completed by Peter

He is ingenious, even artful, for example, the combining of his eating problems with Anticipation Training.

In fact, self-management in depression is very much a matter of gathering up good realistic ideas for future use. Let us now analyse the "Tactics for One-Day Checklist" as completed by Peter in Fig. 2.1 on page 33. The checklist is divided into ten sections, which are organized into a rough time sequence and, with the exception of two, involve a scale, A. B. and C, by which various intensities of difficulty can be noted. Points 7 and 8 differ from the others in that they have no scale but are included as an opportunity for creative ideas.

Point 1: Morning Awakening

For this Peter chose C on the scale of Intensity/ Description and made a small additional note 'very gloomy', meaning he was immediately plunged into a particularly despondent mood. From the note in column three we see that he struck out forcefully at this mood by going for a ten minute jog followed by a sequence of isometric exercises.

Point 2: Routine Depressants

He wrote in a B. Here the point can refer to the activities of a whole day, but Peter has been able to identify one particular regular feature the effects of which he assesses at B, and adds the note "usual nonsense; no parking place. Overnight parkers?" (We need to know more about the special circumstances of Peter's school staff-parking. There used to be parking for early-comers. Now on account of interlopers, there is seldom parking for anybody. It is just this seemingly trivial, routinely-depressing happening which Peter will avoid in future.

Point 3: Stimuli Situations

These can occur randomly throughout the day. Peter gave a

B rating to this specific event, i.e. the moving on, via the demands of the syllabus, to the eighteenth century poets, Cowper, Chatterton et al, all of whom seem to have been exceptionally depressed. Here Peter had his own thought-stopping technique.

Point 4: Other Persons

To this he gave a B. He had a gloomy conversation with a colleague and since this was not a first occurrence he is certain that he is using him as a resonator for the depression. He has decided to make sure he meets him in company in future to avoid this.

Point 5: Feeding Oneself

This point relates to all meals taken during the day. He gave himself a B. In fact he had only two meals, both very scrappy and unappetising. (Here is an opportunity for crossing to a later checklist point because he used this problem as an idea for Activity Scheduling, and if we look at point 7, we shall see precisely how the idea worked.)

Point 6: Upswings

An A rating was given to this category. This refers to one upswing, but any number in a day should be noted. Peter used this optimistic impulse to push forward the specific Activity items in point 7.

Point 7: Anticipation

If required a rating could be inserted here to note the degree of success attained in future events. However, Peter left a blank for no events were anticipated for the day, but some were planned for the future. Thus, he ordered delicatessen for an evening meal, booked a theatre trip.

Point 8: Reinforcements

There is no scale for this, being a note of all reinforcements applied during the day. In this case, Peter reinforced his upswings by sending some research scripts, delayed for completion, to the local adviser for English. Peter has said openly that advisers' careers are "lubricated by teachers' sweat", so he may be expected to seek a substantial reward in due course in the form of a recommendation or a reference etc.

Point 9: Using the Unconscious Mind

Peter has a "Parent" (his dead mother) as big as a house in emotional terms, a manically-ambitious woman, full of jostling schemes for family advancement. Such people can cause their progeny great distress long after they are dead. Peter has her "taped", however, recorded by a woman friend with a similar voice, (Transactional Analysis) and challenges his mother on the tape.

Point 10: Presleeping and Sleeping

Peter has noisy neighbours, who set out for work at 6 a.m. with much revving up. They are also night-jars, coming home in the early hours. Double-glazing does not appeal, but sound-deadening curtains are on the market. Peter has fixed the necessary stronger runners, his wife has made the sound absorbent linings; they both anticipate significantly less disturbance.

Before you set about making up and completing a form for yourself there is one further point to emphasize, the connection with sleeping and pre-sleeping procedures. The best time to complete the form is in the early evening. It means of course that the note on sleeping and pre-sleeping has to be left until the following day. Once you have embarked on this your task must be to analyze the week's rating in the most positive manner. Any Point ratings that are stubbornly refusing to move higher need particular attention. Progress will be patchy.

STAGE OR ACTION	INTENSITY DESCRIPTION	DESCRIPTION OF ACTION/PLAN
1. Morning Awakening		
2. Routine Depressants		
3. Stimuli Situations		
4. Other Persons		
5. Feeding Oneself		
6. Upswings		
7. Anticipation		
8. Reinforcements		
9. Using Unconscious Mind		
10. Presleeping & Sleeping		

Fig. 2.2 Tactics for a One-Day Checklist

The checklist is bound to show checkpoints that bump along with low ratings for weeks, but any gain on any point will be beneficial. Remember to persist with the programme even if at first you don't notice any improvement. The only real test for successful self-management is success and if a single technique works then you should persist with it. For those few who show no sign of progress or for whom the whole thing becomes a burden, group activities would be better.

It will be helpful at this point to examine the Checklist, explaining what is involved, to enable you to explore the various techniques.

Morning Awakening

The first thought on awakening is often a crucial event. The special surroundings of the waking thought have a strange fixing quality, because in the interval between full wakefulness and full sleep the pressures of external stimuli are most weak, critical awareness is absent. The uninterrupted nature of the morning awakening is the decisive fixing factor. Break the establishing routine by getting up and engaging in some distracting activity, in something novel and uncharacteristic -a swim, a run, a task which is swift, easily arranged.

Routine Depressants

A routine depressant is an event which will probably happen and when it does will darken an existing mood. Examples of this could be the morning post which brings news of rejection or failure or the newspaper carrying items of a demoralizing nature. A routine depressant is semi-predicable, and, therefore, its consequences can be minimized. Leaving the house before the post or newspaper arrives, arranging for them to be read later ensures that the impact is immediately lessened.

Stimuli Situations

A stimulus situation is similar to the above in that it involves stimulus and response, but there it ends. For it can occur in almost any situation or time of day. Then a burst of seemingly automatic depressive thoughts force themselves on us. They occur in acts as natural as car-driving or in the midst of a lesson.

Clearly the routine situation can offer the greatest amount of scope for manipulation. If we know that such and such a routine can produce depressive thoughts we can easily take steps to avoid them.

Routines can be varied, broken up or we can force ourselves to concentrate on our tasks within the routine. However, if these thoughts take place outside a routine act or situation, we have two tasks, one to identify the stimulus behind it and find a pattern and, two, to block the impact of the depressive thinking.

The following extract "Anne, a personal history" illustrates how the stimulus control approach can be used to advantage:

* * * * * * * * * *

When Anne became depressed she determined to try to exert some element of stimulus control over her condition. This kind of self-management can often be of great help in producing improvement, but as she knew, it is often difficult to find the precise stimuli needed. She knew that she had to become skilful in the techniques of self-observation to detect those stimuli causing her distress.

She began with the history of her behaviour before the thought or feeling began. 'I thought that depressive thought, and just before it I was in such and such a situation'. And she wrote down the events that occurred in the short period of time, perhaps even a few minutes, before she felt the depressed feeling grow. She soon began to see a pattern in the stimuli. To begin with there was getting up in the morning with a feeling of gloom which was always intensified by the early morning news. The news was almost always generally bad or threatening.

She noticed that at work she was frequently pushed into a deeper depression by people's tones of voice and attitudes - for example, the boss had a particularly sharp way of passing papers over to her for action and very often she noticed that his mouth was drawn up on one side as he did so. She had brooded about this, and so she put it down as a possible stimulus to depression. She made a written note too about the fact that before her lunch she felt particularly depressed for no adequate reason. She conjectured that this stimulus came from inside; she was hungry and therefore her mood was lowered.

After about a fortnight of making observations and notes, Anne was able to separate several kinds of stimuli that seemed to produce undesirable feelings. Several approaches now seemed open to her. She could, for example, avoid a stimulus by substituting something else for it. For instance, when she got up in the morning she never now turned on the radio news; instead she put a tape on, a favourite one. She labelled and relabelled events that occurred at work, including the apparently hurting comments and gestures the boss made. She introduced pauses too; for example, if the boss made any kind of remark she would normally have interpreted as deprecating or discouraging, she would pause before her reaction and say to herself 'I must relabel this in a way which sounds more cheerful and less critical'. She decided to take an earlier lunch, enabling her to pick the best of the menu, and advance her mid-morning break, at the same time ensuring that she ate something then. From this point on Anne began to notice an improvement in her daily mood.

* * * * * * * * *

Stimulus control is not the only technique we can use. Deliberate attempts at thought-stopping are also possible, particularly in circumstances when depression attacks without warning and no routine can be established.

Other Persons

Since depressive people can be very anti-social, it is essential to realize that other people can be vital to one's recovery. Cold-blooded though it may seem, other people can be used as innovators to suggest ideas, to improve the elements of a situation or to act as counsellors.

Feeding Oneself

'I have no appetite'; 'I must eat'; 'If I eat too much, I'll gain weight'; all these are self-statements of depressives. There are many different approaches to coping with this. For Activity Scheduling training, organizing expectancy in foods is easy. A great variety of new or exotic foods are now available. Growing one's own food, albeit in small quantities, is a good way of building up anticipation. Exercises, for example, morning runs, can be appetite-creating.

Upswings

Upswings, in which a period of optimism reigns, can be

most valuable in one's battle against depression. Then, anticipated activities can be arranged and plans can be made which may not be possible at low times because of lack of energy.

Anticipations

Depressed people look backwards. In fact, it seems to dominate. Optimistic anticipations are a vital key to getting rid of depression. Such anticipations can vary; a walk, a holiday, theatre tickets etc. are all guarantees of the future as pleasurable.

Reinforcements

It is possible to link positive thoughts with pleasurable scenes, but a much wider range of reinforcement is available. One important feature is the reinforcement of accidental happenings. If one can recall, for instance, one of the most pleasurable experiences, it can be used as a positive reward. As a consequence of thinking a chain of positive thoughts for three minutes, one can reward oneself in simple ways.

Using the unconscious mind to combat depression

Methods of unconscious management and control are suggested which fall into two categories, Appeasement and Challenge, often forming the initial parts of a self-management programme.

Here are some examples of Appeasement Strategies:

1. Develop interests which satisfy half-acknowledged needs in realistic ways, for example, an urge to control satisfied by involvement in politics.

2. Release half-acknowledged urges by means of

controlled activities, for example, suppressed aggression eased by boxing, fencing etc.

Pre-sleeping and Sleeping

The pre-sleeping period is crucial and manipulable. It is the time for a depressed person to avoid all links or contacts which renew depressive associations. Seeing a significant television play, reading a particular book or allowing the conversation to move towards depressing topics, must be avoided.

2.7 Conclusion

This has been a comprehensively theoretical and practical programme, aimed at providing a basis for solving depressive problems with the help of a daily checklist. Comprehensive though it attempts to be, however, there are still important elements of depression, as seen through our subject, Peter, still unaddressed. Notable amongst these are:

A. His continued MOTIVATION for teaching, and the degree to which it may be enhanced

B. The extent to which MALADROIT MANAGEMENT contributes both to his depression and the morale-levels around him

C. The scope of STAFF-SUPPORT for individual, group or corporate, decisional or remedial activities

In all the other cameos these points will not be explored in any great depth, but in later chapters these and other important areas will be focussed upon, outlining a series of workshops devised especially for staff-counselling, staff support-group and consultancy applications.

In the next chapter the great hurdle of tension and its consequences will be dealt with, and the ways of overcoming its causes and effects will be suggested.

3 TENSION

Introduction

This chapter is designed to combat a range of anxieties caused by tension (viz. Adele, Cameo 4). Here you will find a programme to deal with anxieties in various forms. If you study it with care, follow its suggestions and use your imagination, you will find your worries eased to a marked degree. There is no doubt that anxious people, teachers especially, can help themselves, if they know how. This is a new programme but the techniques in it are not. They have been built up from modern psychological ideas, used by counsellors to help the anxious to help themselves.

You will find that the programme is set out in two sections. The first is to enable you to understand what kind of anxiety you have. The second, using Adele (Cameo 4), as a basis, describes various methods by which different forms can be attacked.

It is advisable to read both sections carefully before beginning to practise your own methods. All that is necessary at this stage is to study the sections thoroughly, incorporate them into your thinking, and then, after you have identified your problem, start to work through your individual programme, day by day, to a successful easing of your anxious state.

Section 1

3.1 Which Anxiety?

The world of worry can be divided up into three main areas:

> Phobias
> Fears
> Tension States

Phobias are accurately described as unreasonable fears; this explains why they are so tenacious; since they are irrational, they cannot be argued away. People usually admit they are irrational fears, but prefer not to try explaining them. Severe phobias, such as panic on contemplating going out, or terror at the sight of a dog, are like their less severe counterparts, not easily explicable, because they are probably fronting for long-forgotten, real terrors.

Phobias can be isolated or exist in groups. They can present major or minor problems. If minor, they can be "got round". If major, they can close down activities almost entirely, completely altering the sufferer's lifestyle. However, most phobias can be overridden. In time, phobias can disappear by themselves or grow so small as to be practically harmless.

By and large a Fear is a feeling of dread in relation to either an existing stimulus or a possible, coming event. Usually, there really is something to be feared, though, generally, not at a level shown by the intensity of the fear. Fears can help to bring about what is feared through tension and loss of effectiveness. They come in many varieties, such as fear of other people, deprivation, financial disaster or disease, but they lack the very sharp definition and irrational content of phobias. Sometimes highly fearful people lack phobias completely.

Such people usually have considerable imaginative capacity, being able to visualize the consequences of an action, to see themselves in a feared situation and to elaborate on all kinds of dubious possible outcomes of a given act. They are often able to maintain three or four fearful scenarios, i.e. personal scripts of future events, usually disastrous, at one time.

Some people also may have to deal with fears which are all in the head, that is, not accompanied by physical feelings. These can be fears of failing, for example. Since they are imagined it is likely that they can be dealt with by means of rational attack.

There are people who were born with relatively unstable nervous systems which over-react even to the normal stresses of life. They usually feel mildly over-wrought most of their lives, though not continually anxious. To observers they appear somewhat weighed-down by responsibilities and decisions, vulnerable to stresses that the average person absorbs almost casually.

Some people report a Tension-state as being 'anxious about being anxious'. Sometimes people suffer from vague, diffused states of tension when they are not quite sure what they are frightened of but certain that they are frightened.

These states can spring out of previous situations of stress. For example, a tension-state might grow out of a six-monthly period when a fearful person has been concentrating on some bodily symptom such as dyspepsia, or headache with no physical origin. In such cases it seems as though the tension-state comes in as a substitute when the original symptom has failed to cope. The original symptom disappears but, as a consequence of its failure, a more generalized form of tension takes its place. Having to check yourself for concentration, day-dreaming etc. is a good example of symptoms of typical tension-states. A sudden spasm of irresistible fear, that is, a panic, can occur inside a tension-state, when one becomes immediately aware of being overwhelmed by dread.

Summing Up

The time has now come to take stock. If you suffer from a phobia, then develop your own programme of progressive desentisization or exposure; this means that you must accustom yourself to the feared situation by stages. First, imagine steps which cause the least discomfort, moving on by stages to those which cause most discomfort, and then, through relaxation techniques, gain the ability to visualize successive scenes without distress. Once feeling more confident about it all, try the same thing in real life until the phobia is conquered.

If general fears, such as an unruly class, are your problem, then you need a form of Anxiety-Management Training (AMT) in which by imaginary rehearsal of the growth of fear, you gradually gain sensitivity to the feelings of unease within you.

This AMT technique operates in the following way. First deep relaxation is achieved and a clear image of contentment built up in the mind's eye and held. After several sessions the process of dropping into relaxation should become automatic. Then you are ready to adopt the next part of the technique, that is, the recall of some event which has caused tension or strain. The introduction of this scene triggers anxiety, at which point a deliberate attempt has to be made to recover full relaxation by switching off the scene and concentrating on building up relaxation again. This process should be repeated until you can switch on and off at will the anxiety scene, returning to full relaxation. Gradually, those cues of tension increase can be picked up and thus you can anticipate the growth of real tension and return to a relaxed state, even when the real events occur.

Low-level fears, without physical accompaniment, you should attempt to rationalize by self-persuasion, but if the problem is a tension-state, then it would be best to practise fairly elaborate daily programmes of relaxation techniques to deal with feelings as they occur.

It is necessary to chart the progress of all problems by means of different record sheets, with the common systematic purpose of listing events, approaches and effects to identify difficulties.

Section 2

3.2 Tackling the Problems

There arc two alternative methods of relaxation to help you in all aspects of anxiety:

1. Training in progressive relaxation

2. Relaxation by suggestion

The choice of which to use is by preference, but only one method should be used at a time. They are alternatives and substitutes in the event of failure.

3.3 Training in Progressive Relaxation

This is a most important procedure and one which should be thoroughly mastered. At first the technique will take some time, but, as you learn, the period taken for inducing deep relaxation will be shortened.

Begin the training by systematically tensing your large-muscle systems, holding them tense until you give the self-command 'Relax!', at which time you let go immediately. If the muscles are first tensed, they will relax more deeply when they are released. Focus all your attention on each muscle-system as you work through the various groups, so that after practice you will not have to tense the muscles first in order to achieve deep relaxation.

3.4 Method

In a very quiet and dimmed room, sit in a comfortable chair, extend the legs and rest the head on the back of the chair. No part of the body should require the use of muscles for support. Close your eyes, then

a) make a fist with your dominant hand and tense the muscles of the hand and forearm until it trembles. Feel the muscles pull across your fingers and lower part of your forearm. Hold this position for 5-7 seconds, and relax. Note how the muscles feel a warmth flow through them as relaxation flows through them (10-20 seconds). Repeat the process. Each time you do this you will relax further until your arm and hand are completely loose with no tension at all (usually 2 - 4 times is sufficient).

b) Tense your right biceps, leaving your hand and forearm on the chair. When you feel your biceps are as completely relaxed as your hand and forearm, proceed to other muscle groups (listed below) in the same manner:

> Left hand and forearm
>
> Left biceps
>
> Muscles of forehead and top of head
>
> Muscles across top of cheeks and upper lip
>
> Jaw muscles and cheeks
>
> Two muscles in front of throat

Muscles below shoulder blades

Abdomen muscles

Muscles of right upper leg

Muscles on bottom of right calf

Right calf

Arch right foot

Repeat for left leg and foot.

If you feel any tension anywhere in your body, repeat the tension-release cycle for that muscle group. It is often helpful to take a deep breath, hold it while tensing muscles, and let go when releasing.

Practise relaxation regularly. Do not work at it for more than fifteen minutes at a time nor twice within any three hour period. Relaxation may be used to promote sleep if practised while lying down. Properly timed, relaxation can be used for a 'second wind' during study.

3.5 Relaxation by Suggestion (a demystified routine)

When you need to relax, say to yourself,

'I know what being relaxed means. I've been relaxed. I remember the feeling of being relaxed.'

Then, arrange the correct position for relaxation. If you have to stand, try to stand against a firm support, let your shoulders sag, your buttocks loosen; ease the tightness of your forehead, neck and jaw. Should you be able to sit, allow yourself to slump, head-forward, eyes half-closed, arms dangling, legs outstretched.

Say to yourself

'This is the beginning of relaxation, the road back to feeling calmer'. Repeat several times.

Then, develop the image of a tension-cloak dropping off your body. A tension-cloak is an imaginary garment, heavy on the shoulders but easy to slip off. Imagine yourself untying it and letting it slip away. Become aware of your breathing. Shut your lips and breathe through the nostrils, listening to the air passing through your nose. Imagine the tension draining away from your body. Start counting steadily, again imagining the tension draining away from your body.

Become self-absorbed, unaffected by outside sounds or promptings from within yourself. Sit in your "centre", absorbed.

In addition to the practice of relaxation there are various other strategies appropriate for coping with various aspects of anxiety and these will be dealt with below.

3.6 Attack on Phobias

It was mentioned earlier that the classical method of attacking a phobia was to desensitize oneself. Figures 3.1 and 3.2 give examples of how desensitization, both for imagination and real life situations, can be organized.

To illustrate this, imagine a youngish man who has a severe lift-phobia. Our intending lift-user built himself the desensitization ladders, see Figures 3.1 and 3.2 on pages 53 and 54.

The figure opposite shows the results of the first phase of imaginary desensitization. (Figure 3.1) He broke his lift-phobia into eight stages, each advancing one step up the ladder of apprehension. When he came to try out his sensitization ladder on an imaginative basis, he put aside two periods for practice, one in the morning and one in the evening. The results of such practice can be seen over a period of about a fortnight, showing the fairly rapid improvement at the start, customary in these cases, a dropping back a little within two days, moving on to a higher plateau and finally achieving a constant, completely desensitized position at the end.

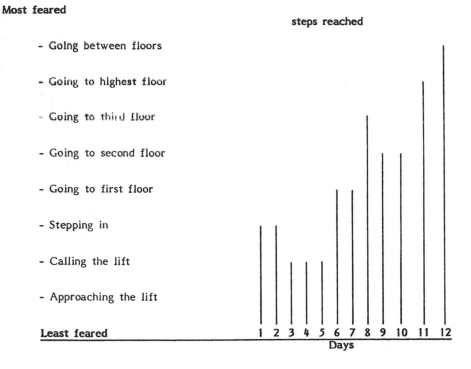

Fig. 3.1   Imagination Ladder

A rather different pattern emerges in Figure 3.2. You would not expect to see immediately successful desensitization in real life, but rather a steady gain maintained at a steady level until by the seventh or eighth week it is almost a complete ladder. Finally after consistent progress in weeks eight, nine and ten, he recorded that he was completely desensitized.

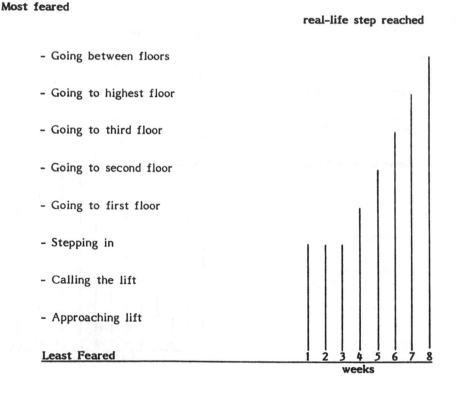

Most feared

real-life step reached

- Going between floors

- Going to highest floor

- Going to third floor

- Going to second floor

- Going to first floor

- Stepping in

- Calling the lift

- Approaching lift

Least Feared

1 2 3 4 5 6 7 8
weeks

Fig. 3.2 Real Life Ladder

Figure 3.2 shows the results when he tried out the various rungs in real life situations. Of course, the second ladder relates to a different time-scale since it is impractical to arrange for the different scaled attempts more than once a day or even on successive days. The real life attempts, which began once he had managed to maintain top rung for seven clear days on the imagination ladder, are based on weekly units, that is, in the course of one week he would attempt the whole scale at different times, trying to edge up rungs from day to day.

How should you proceed along a course of this kind?

First, build your ladder by writing down on separate cards all the steps. Then make charts, using Figs. 3.1 and 3.2 as examples. Then, take the lowest card and begin your relaxation routine. Once completely relaxed, imagine yourself performing the activity of the first step. Note your progress on the chart. Then, review the first step swiftly and repeat the procedure for this second step. It is not important how long the climb takes provided that eventually you succeed in climbing to the top.

After that you can plan for the real life ladder. The lift-phobia can be used as a model for creating a ladder. There are five or more stages of the intensification of the fear involved. For example, there is the approaching of the lift, then calling it, stepping inside and then the movement of the lift to the various floors. This allows for a complete range of intervals to use as rungs on the ladder.

It is obviously impossible to provide a set of ladders suitable for every sort of phobia, since features differ. Anyone trying self-management of a phobia needs to be creative in producing their own ladders.

The method for doing this is quite clear if one asks oneself the "who", the "why", the "which" and the "how" of the phobia, that is under what circumstances it is triggered, what time and the intensities reached all along the way, to the maximum severity of the fear. Every phobia has a sequence and also useful elements, for example, time. Does it build up over time?   Very large numbers of different phobias can be handled by the desensitization method, that is by looking at the feared situation squarely and intelligently.

But this method cannot work in some instances, for example, fear of being unable to control an unruly class, because, in this case, real life rehearsals are difficult. Under situations of this sort you would use the technique of Anxiety Management Training which concentrates upon the development and control of anxiety at an early stage.

3.7 Control of More General Fears

Anxiety Management Training (AMT) uses deep relaxation. In one's deep relaxation a clear image of a scene of contentment and peace is built up in the mind's eye. Several sessions of such relaxation should be followed until the process of dropping into relaxation is automatic.
Once this is achieved you can move on to the next part of the process, the recall of some event which has caused tension or strain. The introduction of this scene triggers anxiety and this is the moment to make a deliberate effort to recover full relaxation by switching off the scene and concentrating upon building up the relaxation again. This process should be repeated again and again until you are practised at switching on and off the scene and returning to full relaxation. As session succeeds session you will become more and more skilful at turning off the tension image. Gradually a proficiency will be built up, that of being able to control situations by switching to relaxation when picking up cues of tension increase. (A.M.T. was developed by Dr. R. Suinn)

The details given on page 57 (1 - 10), and Fig. 3.3 on page 59 gives details of a daily schedule to be adopted.

Prepare two recorded messages:

The first, "Put your mind onto a scene that gave you anxiety. Really put yourself back into the incident."
The second, "Get rid of that scene. Concentrate on your relaxation."

1. Practise relaxation until full relaxation is gained.

2. Relax, developing a clear image of a peaceful, comfortable event.

3. Practise relaxing and developing the image in order to relax further. Vary the image if necessary.

4. Use the tape-recorded message "Move on to a scene that gave anxiety. Really put yourself back into the incident."

5. Switch on the second recorded message when feeling the anxiety "Get rid of that scene. Concentrate on your relaxation."

6. Practise this technique of dismissing the image and returning to the relaxed state. Observe how the anxiety develops, its location and pattern.

7. Concentrate on the "dismissed and returning to the relaxation" phase.

8. Begin a relaxation/anxiety image session, but instead of cutting off the anxiety before it develops, let it build. Then cut it back to relaxation and switch off scene.

9. Practise the big build-up and cut-back.

10. Observe yourself in real life situations where anxiety is generated. Note tendencies to cut back to a calmer, controlled posture, as soon as you are becoming tense.

Go on practising AMT until you can at will shift to controlled relaxation in any real life situation that produces anxiety.

3.8 Tackling Tension-States and Panics

Fear of fear, in the absence of any good reason for it, or a general tension and pre-occupation with seemingly trifling thoughts and feelings, are typical of tension states. With the help of Adele (cameo 3) we can develop a checklist to act as a guide/assessment by means of a scale A, B, C, as previously, and a long-term record of attempts to modify a tension-state by self-help methods.

The completed chart on page 59, fig. 3.3, is the mid-process record of a woman who has been suffering from a tension state for about two months, and who has managed to establish a degree of proficiency in relaxation. She is keen to see all her ratings in the chart at an A level within a reasonable time. All her lifestyle is tailored, in a sense, to easing this; she is alert to every possibility of keeping up the high levels and jacking up the low. At present her overall ratings on the A B C scale are, as depicted, all in the A B category with no Cs visible.

She intends to bring them all to an A standard. Fig. 3.4 on page 61 gives the Checklist details for anyone wishing to use it.

3.9 Discussion of Adele's Daily Checklist

1. Pre-rising Relaxation

It is vital to make a calm start to the day. A routine relaxation phase should be tried each morning.

As soon as Adele awoke, the odd, uneasy feelings came back, but she has a very capable and swift relaxation technique to combat these.

2. Concentration (1)

Maintaining concentration on a given task is one of the most difficult problems facing a sufferer from a tension state, but various techniques can be employed to assist concentration.

1. Pre-rising relaxation	B	Felt a quick return to tension on waking, but lay a while, did some exercises and made some auto-suggestions.
2. Concentration (1)	B	Lost my thread several times during the double-period, but was able to challenge very successfully. Observed more intense note-taking as a consequence.
3. Mid-Morning Activities	A	Found myself a quiet corner and ran through all my relaxation routine, together with the suggestions.
4. Panics	B	Felt the beginnings of a panic at about 12.15, but managed to create an "island", study my card and catch a glimpse of myself. It was not a serious episode.
5. Rhythm Phase	B	Listened to one of my "quietening" tapes in car at lunchtime. Felt for the rhythm and allowed myself to be lulled and soothed.
6. Concentration (2)	B	Put out my heading cards boldly and used the lab-timer to sequence me through. This new regime is having some interesting impacts in the class.
7. Evening Stimuli	A	Having left spouse his supper, I repaired to the local CLP meeting where I laid into the Secretary about p.c. selection arrangements being undemocratic.
8. Presleeping & Sleeping	B	Went through the presleeping routine, had a "night-start" but got off; woke at about 4 am, did some exercises and got off again about 5 am. Slept well, despite waking and, paradoxically, felt fresh.

Fig. 3.3 Daily Checklist for a Tension State (Adele)

Despite great familiarity with the material, she found herself, occasionally, losing the thread of her discourse, and once or twice, actually at a loss for words. When this happened, she boldly challenged the class to supply the words she sought, or to pin-point the exact stage reached in the lesson. This shift, from the didactic to the socratic, took the class unawares, and had the salutary effect of increasing its concentration and intensifying its note taking. How frequently she will be able to use this tactic remains arguable; she will not be able to overwork it.

3. Mid-morning Activities

Some opportunity for internal retreat is essential if a Tension-state is to be eased.

At some time during the middle of the morning she found a quiet corner and ran through the repertoire of relaxation exercises, complete with suggestions. This is her routine and its success does depend upon not being observed. Her mid-morning activities are very successful and she rates them A.

4. Panics

It's important to realise that the usual meanings attached to the word "panic" bear no resemblance to the experience of real panic. Special strategies are necessary for panic-prone teachers. Panic can attack at the most inconvenient moments (in a lesson's fullest flow, with all eyes on the teacher).

Therefore the first tactic to adopt is the forward planning of "islands", that is, a spot in time and place where the teacher can linger, relatively unobserved. For example, you can say to the class 'I've forgotten something ...' or 'Now's the moment for you to ...'. The "island" thus created gives the opportunity for a glance at a panic list, a model of which can be found at the end of the chapter, on page 64.

Point	Assessment	Note
1. Pre-rising Relaxation		
2. Concentration (1)		
3. Mid-morning Activities		
4. Panics		
5. Rhythm Phase		
6. Concentration		
7. Evening Stimuli		
8. Presleeping & Sleeping		

Fig. 3.4 Example of Individual Checklist

At about 12.15, for no very clear reason, she felt the beginnings of a panic. She started to feel strange and alienated and to wonder if she were about to break out into wild, insane shouting. All this in the middle of a demanding GCSE Chemistry lesson in the laboratory. Fortunately, a cupboard-search offered her the opportunity to create an "island", and she was able to glance at her Panic List and to catch a glimpse of her calm-appearing self in the reflection of the cupboard door. The lesson, an extended experiment, conveniently let itself be "put on hold" for a few minutes while the panic lasted. When she came out from the "island", nobody seemed to notice her gazing absently into space, ostensibly waiting for the appropriate moment to move on to a further phase of the experiment.

5. Rhythm Phase

She is always on the look out for rhythm phases. On this day she finds one in a lunch-time tape. She leans back, sandwich in hand, and lets herself drift into the rhythms of the music. She finds the whole exercise lulling and soothing. Since, however, she still finds herself with odd apprehensive feelings, she rates the experience B.

6. Concentration (2)

She is an experienced teacher, with an exceptional grasp of lesson-sequence. Nevertheless she does not hesitate to buttress her concentration, constantly under threat from reverie, with a meticulously organized set of cue cards, with the experimental steps headlined. These she has bound into a flip-over format and set up the laboratory timer to cue her through the sequence, resetting it at every card.

7. Evening Stimuli

Evenings can be tricky and painful episodes. So, she tends to build up an advance programme of distraction to nullify such events. In this case, she sees to her husband's needs and then sets out for her constituency party meeting where, she was active in thwarting the secretary's manoeuvres to have the National Executive's nominee preferred over a local woman for prospective parliamentary candidate. Expressing anger and the release of frustration on to a relatively safe object can be a cathartic technique of great effectiveness, lifting mood and giving the mind an invigorating buzz for a Tension State, as explained through the character, Adele.

8. Pre-sleeping and Sleeping

She came in fairly late and retired immediately. Because she had driven some distance, her pre-sleeping relaxation routine proved incapable of preventing her from dropping off quickly, and soon was roused by a sudden nightmare with the visual accompaniment of "seeing" herself heading for a crash. She woke with a start, but immediately, in a sleepy automatic way began to practise her sleeping relaxation routine and was able to drop back to sleep within minutes. She rated the night B and continues to use the pre-sleeping and sleeping routine as described.

Now that you have studied the notes on the checklist you are now ready to self-manage the list.

The would-be self manager with a tension state should copy the checklist (Fig. 3.4 page 61), making at least 300 copies to cover a daily assessment of 300 days.

The checklist should be completed at the end of each day or, as in point 8, the next morning.

It acts as a constant incentive to subdue this, the objectives being to attain a continuous sequence of checklists with exclusively A assessments.

Panic List

1. I have had this panic before and nothing happened.
2. A minute ago I thought I was going to die (or go mad), but here I am, not dead/mad.
3. This panic will go the way of all other panics: grow, peak, fade and vanish.
4. There is nothing in this panic beyond an exaggeration of normal body sensations.
5. You have a kit of thought-stopping, relaxation techniques; now is the time to use it.
6. All you have to do is to act, and wait.
7. Try to **plan** your attack on the panic.
8. As soon as the attack begins to fade, start to think about the task it interrupted.
9. The number and intensity of your panics is diminishing; perhaps this will be the last.

To maintain the precision and tenacity of this anti-panic attack, the list should be typed out on to a small card so that it can be held like a playing card in the hand or interleaved in a book.

The aim throughout this chapter has been to encourage individuals to self manage their tensions, particularly through relaxation, no easy thing today. In the next chapter we shall see how the art of relaxation continues to play an important part in the fight against stress.

4 HABITS AND OBSESSIONS

4.1 Introduction

As in the previous chapter, we shall make use of the characters in the cameos to help us to understand problems brought on by or caused by symptoms of stress and to plan their destruction. This chapter is aimed at helping teachers to rid themselves of compulsive symptoms, tics, bad habits and obsessions which are so devastating to those who suffer from them. They are grouped together here because their self management is similar and can therefore be tackled together. First, though, let us have a brief description of each.

4.2 Symptoms

A. Tics

The tic is a spasmodic, nervous habit, with no physical cause, most often occurring as a facial twitch, but which can also be found in other parts of the body, hand, shoulder etc..

These tics can come and go, or be a constant problem,

affecting different nerve and muscle systems. They can cause serious occupational difficulties for those afflicted, even though they are usually painless. This is particularly the case for teachers and anyone else involved in presentation.

B. Habits

Habits share some of the qualities of tics and obsessions. They consist of a regular, repetitive piece of behaviour. Addictions to smoking, alcoholism, drugs, over-eating etc. all lie within the definition of the bad habit. Unlike tics and obsessions, however, bad habits of the kind mentioned above could be potentially catastrophic, undermining all prospects of promotion, happiness and well-being.

C. Obsessions

Obsessions are of two main groups - the "Having to do" and the "Having to think" kinds.

The "Having to do" are usually of the checking or verifying kind. Such rituals, mild, moderate or severe, can exist in isolation or in groups, being a form of repetitive behaviour, designed to safeguard the checker against his actions or the actions of others. An example of this is the repeated checking of lights, fires, stoves, doors etc. before retiring. In mild cases, such checking repetitions are repeated once or twice. But in severe forms this ritual is persistent, blocking other activities and often coercing other people into the ritual behaviour.

The "Having to think" kind takes the form of tunes, phrases or images which come into the mind unbidden and cannot be expelled. Obsessions seem to stem from anxiety, not a simple direct one but an attempt to prevent loss of control by a very rigorous regime of diversion and regulation. Obsession too creates its own secondary anxieties, for example, the feeling of loss of control that the obsession engenders, and can in severe cases turn to panic.

Conclusions

Tics, habits and obsessions are of course symptoms of a special kind. Usually, when we speak of a symptom we mean a signal of alarm to which we respond by ridding ourselves of the causes. Tics, habits and obsessions are symptoms in this sense. Therefore, it follows that they should be eliminated. To this end all the resources of Workshops, given in the latter chapters of this book, may be used to distract, occupy, etc. the conflicts and difficulties that may operate to build up new symptoms.

4.3 Elimination

A) Tics

One method of eliminating tics is known as "the pairing-technique". It works in the following way:

1. Ask someone to observe the tic closely and give you a clear description of its appearance, by writing it down or drawing it.

2. Recruit two or three observers to collaborate in the self management by observing the frequency. Issue them with charts (see Fig. 4.1 page 68)

3. Rehearse tic movement six sessions daily at two-hour intervals. Simulate twelve movements per session and note trials on a chart (see Fig. 4.2 page 69)

4. Continue this for two months

5. At the end of each week, check progress with observers of the frequency of noticing the real tic.

	Mon.	Tues.	Wed.	Thurs.	Fri.	Sat.	Sun.
am. seen							
est.							
pm. seen							
est.							

This chart is not as simple as it appears. It is divided into the number of tics seen a.m. and p.m., and the number estimated to have occurred.

Tics seen is a fraction of tics estimated when **time available to observe** is allowed for, i.e. if there is little opportunity to observe, but the frequency is high, the estimation will be high.

Fig. 4.1 Tic Frequency Chart

If there is a considerable lessening, persist until the real tic is negligible. If only a slight lessening is noticed, then try combining this method with intensive relaxation method.

Mon. Tues. Wed. Thurs. Fri. Sat. Sun.

**Session
    no.**

_____

**Session
    no.**

_____

To complete this chart, note the sessions nos.
1-6 in the day column.

Fig. 4.2 Recording chart for personal use

The chance to practise relaxation needs to be grasped
when the opportunity arises.

Variations in relaxation routines is therefore valuable. A
relaxation method, which will not necessarily fit a
snatched, informal situation, may serve very well in a
planned and timetabled setting.

Figure 4.3 on the next page is an example of a daily
timetable of pairing and relaxation.

AM

Formal relaxation	e.g. just before rising
Informal relaxation	e.g. on train/bus
Pairing practice	e.g. in rest room
Informal relaxation	e.g. in lunch break

PM

Pairing practice	e.g. in rest room
Informal relaxation	e.g. on train/bus
Formal relaxation	e.g. after an evening meal
Pairing practice	e.g. just before retiring

Fig. 4.3 Combination relaxation and pairing routine

This kind of combination programme offers a great deal of flexibility in attack. If the frequency of the tic by observation still stubbornly refuses to fall, vary the combinations or step up the formal relaxation.

B) Habits

The problem of "Heavy Drinking" will be used here to serve as an example of a self management programme for habit control.

A multi-strategy approach is offered here so that would-be self managers can be both flexible and selective, first trying out all strategies and then choosing and reinforcing those which seem most effective. To show how those with other Habit problems can adapt parts of this multi-strategy to suit their own problems, an adaptation for teachers whose smoking has run out of control, is given later.

Figure 4.4. on page 74 serves two purposes; it gives an outline of the anti-drinking tactics and serves as a framework for a weekly check.

The various strategies are analysed below one by one for you to study before embarking upon them.

1.   **Substitutes**

What is a substitute? Heavy drinking is, in part, often some kind of substitute activity. In place of love, success etc. excessive drinking takes place. Here a range of substitutes is recommended such as soft drinks, mints etc. to fill the need to drink, chew nibble etc. and are less harmful.

2.   **Contracts**

Contracts and contracting is the method by which the alcoholic seeks to reduce his intake of alcohol by a predetermined amount, and, if successful, retrieves money or other valuables placed in the care of a friend. If, on the other hand, he or she fails to meet the target, then it is forfeited with the inconvenient consequences which follow.

3.   **Distractions and Stimuli**

These are key aspects of the programme. An alcohol addict must insulate him or herself from all the various stimuli that previously cued drinking. It is particularly useful to be sensitive and alert to different stimuli for drinking. The examples which follow show some of the stimuli which can be external or internal. For instance, tension or boredom are internal, offer of a drink or a working lunch are external.

Examples of Stimuli:

I will not become involved in "treating", knowing that this will increase my drinking.

I will acquaint myself with "happy hours" in local hotels and pubs, so that I can avoid such times.

I will switch off TV programmes in which drunkennesss is minimised, nor will I watch adverts.

I will programme my day so that I am never left alone with nothing to do but drink.

4.   **Coverants**

Coverant control of alcoholism is a method of self-instruction which involves the repetition of warning statements to the self, following a systematic method. First, the self-manager must keep a record of drinking and impulses to drink. Fig. 4.5 on page 75 shows the method of keeping the record, with the figures 1 - 5 providing a scale showing the intensity of the drinking urge,

1 being the least and 5 the most intense urge. In the record there should be sufficient numbers and spaces to show a full day's drinking urges and actual drinks. It is a good idea to keep this record simultaneously with the record shown in Fig. 4.4.

Next must be the establishment of a routine in which the drinker uses the urge to drink as a stimulus for Coverant control of an urge to drink. That is whenever an urge to drink arises, the drinker must repeat to himself an anti-drinking idea or statement and immediately follow it with a pro-non-drinking statement. The anti-drinking statement should relate to the dangers or disadvantages of drinking, for example, 'You will lose your driving licence through drinking' etc. and the pro-non-drinking statement to positive advantages of stopping drinking. After such statements the self-manager should reward himself with the promise of a pleasurable event.

This coverant routine must become automatic, with the would-be non drinker first experiencing an impulse to drink, then issuing an anti-drinking statement which is followed immediately by the pro-non-drinking statement. He finally moves on to the self-reward.

Substantial numbers of comparable statements should be developed, for each would-be self manager needs at least four of each kind of statement. These should be written down and learned in the order to be followed in the actual self-management programme itself. The originators of this technique, Homme and Danaher, point out the uselessness of taking the statement simply as a recital of intent repeated automatically, ignoring the actual feelings and events which surround the coverant process. They recommend that immediate distractions are suspended and the self statements concentrated on,

End of week date ....

1. Substitutes (my substitute this week) total ....

2. Contracts. I contracted £ ..... for ....
   reduction and won/lost,

3. Distractions & Stimuli.

   I note the following
   alterations in stimuli for
   drinking
   ....
   ....

4. Coverants.

   I performed my coverant
   ..... times

   I missed my coverant
   ..... times

5. Exercises

   I maintained the following
   routine without a break
   ....
   ....

6. Training

   I practised the following
   self-management scheme
   in respect of ....
   note inadequacies and
   scheme.

Fig. 4.4 Substitutes, Contracts, Distractions, Coverants, Exercises & Training Schedule to be completed

using them as cues to bring up the real connections with emotions and feelings about the drinking problem which has motivated one towards self-management.

Date

_____

Amount drunk -
Morning

_____

Amount drunk -
Afternoon &
Evening

_____

Urges to drink
number

_____

Intensity of
urges on scale
least to most
1 - 5

_____

To be completed daily, liquor only, not substitutes

Fig. 4.5 Drinking Schedule

6. Exercises

The heavy drinker is usually short of good physical exercise and the feeling of relaxation and well-being it can bring. Exercise is invaluable both as a counter-thrust to, and a substitute for, drinking. A substantial amount of the heavy drinker's day can be absorbed by exercises of one kind or another. Mild exercise routines start the process off and after a while, provided one is fit (and one's potential fitness must be known first) more intensive and demanding programmes can be developed.

Exercises can be divided up into two main groups, A) agility and B) endurance. A mixture of the two is recommended, devised according to preference. These will be found in Fig. 4.6 (agility type) on page 77 opposite and in Fig. 4.7 (endurance type) on page 78.

(Before beginning this course of exercises, all self-managers should check with their family practitioner to establish their potential fitness.)

Leisure Counselling

The purpose of leisure counselling is the deliberate programming of an activity in order to block, thwart or weaken comprehensively a habit. Such a programme is best attempted with an activity that

a) permits a multi-angle, multi-phase attack on the habit

b) can be subjectively reinforced by the habit-sufferer

c) can be flexibly implemented by agreement between the leisure-counsellor and the sufferer.

Leisure-counselling selects swimming as an optimal opponent against heavy drinking because for example, developing an interest in swimming may benefit him or her psychologically from the soothing experience of warm immersion; may build up non-alcohol-promoting social contacts etc.

Agility type exercises	appropriateness summer	winter

Several advantages.

1) increase muscle tone

Tennis ✓
Badminton ✓ (winter)

2) decrease feelings of
weakness/stiffness

Squash ✓ (winter)
Racquets ✓ (winter)
Basketball ✓ (winter)
Sailing ✓ (summer)

3) Offer solid, social
contacts, not drinking
contacts

others

They **must** be phased in
in easy stages. e.g.
Tennis:

first week and subsequent
two weeks - 2 sets per week
3-6 weeks - 3 sets per week
6-9 weeks - 3 sets twice weekly

Fig. 4.6 Exercise Notes A – Agility

Endurance type exercises		appropriateness summer	winter
Several advantages			
1) absorb time	cycling	✓	✓
	jogging (must	✓	✓
2) increase appetite for food	follow walking proficiency)		
3) produce pleasant fatigue	walking	✓	✓
	swimming	✓	✓
	climbing	✓	
4) build up cardio-vascular tone (but must be phased in)	others		

They **must** be phased in
in easy stages e.g.

Cycling:

1st day and 7 subsequent days	– two miles only
7–14 days	– four miles
14–28 days	– six miles
28 days plus	– sustained eight miles

Fig. 4.7 Exercise Notes B – Endurance

7. Training

Many heavy drinkers have a range of problems, social, vocational or domestic that keep up their excessive use of alcohol. If these problems involve a lack of skill in, for example, assertiveness, social tactics, job-securing etc. then building up such skills on a basis of self-training may enable the heavy drinker to shrug off the causes.

Training may well involve the building up of parallel programmes almost as extensive as the overall habit itself. The self-manager has to make his or her own decision about the weight of effort to place on this part of the programme. He must decode how much to throw into the campaign against the possible causes and how much against the symptom.

Bearing all the previous discussion in mind, now start to develop and complete this anti-drinking campaign. Figure 4.8 on page 80, illustrating Gillian's (cameo 5) campaign, can be used as a guide.

Make a list of all purchasable soft drinks.

Systematically begin a daily intake of these. Note them in the substitutes panel. (Make sure the soft drinks do not act as a stimuli for "real drinking", i.e. do not consume them in a "real" drink setting).

Start weekly contracts for realistic reductions of drinking amounts. Attempt to reduce drinking by contract.

At the same time identify as many stimuli to drinking as possible. Eliminate it immediately and generate a distraction (some pleasurable event, for example).

Substitutes	My Substitutes:	12 pints of soft drinks, non-alcoholic shandies, cordials, gingers and apple juice.20 packets of assorted sweets; mints, toffees, gum etc. spread through the week.

Contracts   I contracted £10.00 for
a 15% wine reduction, and
won.

**Distractions/
Stimuli**   I altered car route to
dodge beer hoarding. Went
round shopping precinct to
avoid passing off-licence.

Coverants   I performed my coverant, not
regularly, but according to
drinking urge.

Exercises   Am swimming at the half-mile
level, total for one week -
4 miles.

Training   I practised the following self-
management schemes in respect
of changing my job, i.e. I practised
job-interview responses, and updated
my curriculum vitae to show to
would-be employers.

**Fig. 4.8 Substitutes, Contracts, Distractions, Coverants,
Exercises and Training Schedule
Completed by Gillian in a Week**

Complete the Drinking Schedule on a daily basis and also note the number of urges to drink; this should be followed each time by reciting one's coverant phrases mentioned earlier.

At the same time begin a graded exercise, using it also as a time-filler as well as an invigorator. The least sign of overfatigue should be a sign to reduce the exercise load.

Now begin to build up a training programme to improve your assertiveness or whatever you have decided on is causing your condition. There are many ways of developing your programme. Briefly they involve defining/stating objectives, sorting our appropriate strategies to achieve this, selecting relevant techniques and devising methods of recording progress.

Keep the running records carefully and scrutinize them constantly. Thorough scrutiny will reveal useful changes towards greater drinking control. Positive factors should be carefully reinforced, ideas and strategies tried.

Another example of a self-management programme for habit-control is in the multi-strategy approach to the management of smoking. I have selected this particular Habit because it is the most hazardous to health. This multi-strategy can be flexible and selective: all can be tried, then selected, then the most effective reinforced.

Fig. 4.9 on page 82 can be used in two ways, first as a description of strategies to be adopted and secondly, as a checklist; Fig. 4.10 on page 83 shows how to make up a daily and weekly chart. The strategies are as described earlier in the chapter for Drinking strategies.

	End of week date ....
1. Substitutes	My substitutes total .....
2. Contracts	I contracted (state sum or valuable) .... for .... and won/lost
3. Distractions & Stimuli	I note the following alterations in stimuli for smoking ....
4. Coverants	I performed my coverant .... times
5. Exercises	I maintained the following routine without a break ....
6. Training	I practised the following self-management scheme in respect of .... (note inadequacies and scheme)

Fig. 4.9 Substitutes, Contracts, Distractions, Coverants, Exercises and Training Schedule to be Completed Weekly

	Mon.	Tues.	Wed.	Thurs.	Fri.	Sat,	Sun.
Substitutes							
Contracts							
Smoking urges & cigarettes	am pm	am pm	am pm	am pm	am pm	am pm	am pm
Coverants performed							
missed							
Exercises							
Training							
Notes							

Fig. 4.10 Daily and Weekly Chart

As in the Drinking schedule shown earlier, a record as shown in Fig. 4.11 must be kept daily, using a scale 1-5 showing the intensity of smoking.

Date ....

No. of cigarettes smoked,
                    morning ....

No. of cigarettes smoked,
                    afternoon ....

Urges to light up, number ....

Intensity of urges,
on scale least to most 1-5 ....

Fig. 4.11 Smoking Schedule

C. Obsessions

As said earlier the world of Obsessions is divided up into "Having to do" and "Having to think" rituals. There are those who are plagued with a combination of both, however, and for these a combination of programmes is recommended. Let us start with a systematic attack on "Having to do" rituals. The programme consists of four aspects, as follows

1.   Practising the ritual from "cold", i.e. when it

is not triggered by an urge or happening;

2.   Continuously observing the normal reaction to tormenting stimulus, for example, a dog stroked without the compulsive-hand washing which follows;

3.   Relaxation/pleasure phase in which the self-manager fills his or her mind with compensating interests and sensations;

4.   Ritual Management Practice, a variation of AMT, in which, in imagination, the self-manager practises switching the ritual on and off and thereby develops a substantial degree of control over it.

Participation in a Relaxation Workshop either individually or in a group is recommended as a self-help exercise. More will be said about group Workshops later. Indeed the later part of the book has been deliberately given over to the use of workshops to help in the conquering of Stress in its various parts. As a self management routine the Ritual Management Practice should be adopted twice a day for a month. As has been said earlier, it is a variation of AMT, described in chapter 2, but the aim is to rid oneself of the ritual.

The "Having to think" ritual can take many forms, but there are, usually, three main types, unacceptable images, repetitive phrases, or repetitive tunes. Their effectiveness varies from frightening to tiresome, from totally-distracting to marginally attention-catching. There seem to be certain causes; the greater the degree of fear they provoke, the more they persist; they can be set off by a range of stimuli, stress, increased responsibilities etc.; they can and do break into periods of relative inactivity; they are dependent to a degree on the maintenance of a larger lifestyle ritual, embracing the whole pattern of the sufferer's activities. New surroundings, new circumstances can lessen them.

Although sufferers may be tempted to despair there are many good reasons for optimism. We find that even the most persistent ritual will end after a while. It is possible to maintain a good level of concentration, even during the most persistent of obsessive thoughts. Given the right motivation, all things are possible, and stress can be conquered. The theme will be continued in the next chapter when we discuss the renewing of one's creativity.

5 RENEWING CREATIVITY AND RESTORING MEMORY

5.1 Introduction

Creativity and Memory are both cognitive powers. As was revealed in chapter one, Stress can have a daunting or even devastating effect on both one's Creativity and Memory. On the face of it these two have no connection, but in fact they are related through their cognitive aspects, although each causes somewhat different problems.

An enormous quantity of interest has been generated around the subject of creativity. Although it has been claimed that there are specific ages for peak creative performance (youthful poets and mathematicians, for example,) such studies are based on highly selective data, derived from easily obtained biographical sources of famous personalities. However, even these specialized theories have often been upset by contrary evidence of a striking kind (for example, sexagenarian poets and octogenarian composers).

Variation in creative phases depends very much upon mood, motivation and technique, the absence of which in any combination can cause an objective decline in original thinking. Re-energizing one's apparently diminished creative powers is a challenge requiring both skill and guile, combined with a certain ruthlessness, as we shall see when we work through the techniques tried by Frank (cameo 6).

As Jack in cameo 7 showed, memory-lapse causes somewhat different problems. We take memory for granted, unmindful that it is a phenomenal gift, providing us with our special sense of identity and continuity.

Since both diminished creative powers and memory lapses are often brought on by attributable consequences, it is the purpose of this chapter to work on the prevention and/or cure by means of our self management guide.

5.2 Renewing One's Creativity

It is fundamental to realize that creativity does not mean simply originality. Virtually everything has a precursor. It is surprising to realize, for instance, that Milton's *Lycidas*, one of the most famous elegies in English Literature, contains several phrases which have been lifted from a normally-excluded book of the Bible.

One might say that creativity is heavily-worked adaptability. It is old data blended together, legitimately transformed to fit a fresh context and therefore made new. In fact, we can see the logic of this theory of creativity, if we consider that the material can only consist of ideas in words, numbers or diagrams, their only source and origin.

It is important to question such statements as "inspiration is 95% perspiration". Those Professionals who live by "creative" output usually work within a context of previous acceptability and can justify such a style far more easily than those who may need every scrap of inspirational boost to gain acceptance.

The rhythms of creativity are, therefore, important and need to be taken into account. They are, however, only one tactic in a style strategy which in fact contains eleven in all. These tactics are described below.

Tactics

1. Experiment seriously with a prescribed tactic, such as Twilight technique (see section 5.3); Searchings etc.

2. Start a diary or common-place book, to trap any passing idea of note.

3. Begin to act creatively again by small steps, for example, write a single sentence, conceive part of a design each day, to build to bigger units of achievement.

4. Try to build up a large credit-balance on ideas/style, by reading, studying, observing and discussing extensively.

5. Seize an inspirational rhythm and exploit it without restraint.

6. Review past creative achievements positively.

7. Focus on anecdotes of mature, creative achievers.

8. Try techniques to start inspirational flow, for example, jogging, meditating etc.

9. Develop a calm "centre of confidence", from which creativity can flow.

10. Remember that creativity is the product of a flow of ideas and the skill to dip into it selectively.

Sooner or later, those two must be present and interactive.

11. Have a creative objective in mind, not too focussed initially as to interfere with motivation.

Frank (cameo 6) set out a weekly programme aimed at renewing his creativity, using tactics mentioned above.

His actions are set out in Fig. 5.1. on page 91.

5.3 The Twilight Technique (i.e. subliminal recovery)

There are two twilight periods.

The first may occur in that brief interval between waking and sleeping. Into that comfortable margin, when one's head is on the pillow and one is relaxed but not yet asleep, intrude thoughts which have the shape of semi-reality. They can be very simple: a familiar voice, a melody; they can be elaborate: a street scene in full animation.

The second may happen at the other end of the night, sleeping to waking time, with very similar phenomena. However, since there is usually more light, some images may be projected on to surrounding objects with bizarre results. A bedside clock may seem to tell the wrong time; a speck on the ceiling may move like an insect.

These differ from dreams in one very important aspect, that is, they are flexible. A scene can be changed, a design altered etc. Nor are they usually fresh experiences; they may have occurred often in childhood, although now long forgotten.

These states have one invaluable feature; they are freed from the inhibitions and conventions of thinking which govern waking thoughts. Such a freedom offers an open window into memories blocked off, to lines of reasoning disrupted, and to

	Mon	Tues	Wed	Thurs	Fri	Sat
Tactics		Tried Twilight		Tried Searching		Tried Twilight
Diary	Idea Noted	Idea Noted			Idea Noted	
Shifts			Did a quick sketch			
Credit	Read & took notes		Read & took notes			
Rhythm				Found a rhythm & completed sketch		
Review					Thought about my sixties poetry	
Focus	Read about Goethe		Read about Thos. Hardy			
Techniques				Jogging		Jogging
Develop					Tried for calm centre	
Remember						Tried flow & selection

Fig. 5.1 Weekly Programme to Renew Frank's Creativity

emotional colours faded. If, though, that state is allowed to run on aimlessly, passing from one image to another, no problem-solving, creativity-gaining benefits accrue. This does not mean that every opportunity ought to be exploited. They must be wooed intelligently and sensitively. What is needed is an operational checklist for anyone attempting this kind of imagery. Although not everyone can recover this childhood capability, it is very worthwhile making the attempt.

Such a checklist might be as follows:

> Some preparation is required, that is, try to frame the problem mentally in advance, and find an easily available recording method. A tape recorder by one's bedside is invaluable for those who make their notes verbally. For those whose ideas come in the form of diagrams, mathematics or technical notes, paper and pen should be at hand.

> As soon as you sense a solution, an idea, rouse yourself fully to record either on tape or in note form, then say to yourself 'that's an achievement' and go back to sleep.

> On rising, review your notes, and expand them during the day. You may find that only part of the problem has been solved. This is the time to say reassuringly to your subconscious 'so far, so good. But I can go further, perhaps not now, but soon.'

5.4 Key-word Searching

One of the traditional methods of applied imagination, ranging back over at least three millennia, and endorsed by creative thinkers as widely diverse as Socrates and Rudyard Kipling, has been key-word searching.

Association is the name of this creative game. Association

is driven by words or concepts which can be drawn or performed. It is the powerhouse of thinking and undoubtedly much of it goes on at levels of the mind we cannot plumb. As we all know, one thing can, and does, lead to another. We need a set of clearly explained methodologies to make association work to order. The first of these is the Thesaurus method.

5.5 The Thesaurus Method

Roget's *Thesaurus* is, as you know, a dictionary of synonyms, cross-referenced for a large number of words in various categories.

Here is a good example to work through. Let us imagine that we have to devise the Publicity for an Exhibition of Handicrafts to be held in school. Under the word Publicity in the Thesaurus, we find a range of synonyms and related terms, for example,

a) Press;	b) Newspaper;
c) Periodical;	d) Journal;
e) Gazette;	f) House Organ;
g) Trade Publication;	h) Tabloid;
i) Daily, Weekly, Monthly;	j) Annual;
k) Monograph;	l) Book;

and so on

These immediately throw up an enormous variety of ideas:

f), for example; Is it possible to use the magazines of local firms in the area to promote the Exhibition?

And there is g); could we get Trade Publications interested. Could we persuade Handicraft firms to advertise in a special magazine?

Already our once meagre source of ideas is growing.

This is only the beginning of the systematic search. The first group was drawn from the *Thesaurus* list of Nouns. Suppose we move into other categories, for example, Verbs, Adverbs etc., each sparking off as yet undiscovered notions.

Up till now, too, only one third of the task is completed. Only "Publicity" has been searched; there is still "Exhibition" and "Handicrafts" waiting to be tackled in the same way. This invaluable method is put to use again in what is known as the synonyms method.

5.6 Synonyms Method

This is more comprehensive in its approach, employing the *Thesaurus* to make a total transformation of the wording of a given problem. The transformation, which can involve both word and phrase, might result in something like the example given below.

* * * * * * * * * *

Stated Problem: an untypical, technical challenge.

"Rough ground/ causes body distortion/ in vehicles/ with rigid/ wheel mountings".

Transform	Transformation Number
Rough ground to **uneven surface**	1
Body distortion to **chassis dislocation**	2
Vehicles to **carriers**	3
Rigid to **stiff**	4
Wheel mountings to **wheel attachments**	5

1. The word "surface" suggests a vehicle that will ride above the surface of the rough ground like an airship.

2. This phrase gives a connotation of a movement in the frame and suggests a jointed chassis.

3. The word carriers widens the field of possible vehicles.

4. This suggests nothing likely to be useful in solving the problem.

5. Attachments has a quality of flexibility about it and hints at variable position wheel attachments to conform with surface undulations.

When we see the problem restated, we find a kind of solution appearing. Now a different type of vehicle, perhaps revolutionary in design, is being envisioned and development outlined.

The problem restated is:

"Uneven surface causes chassis dislocation to carriers with stiff wheel attachments".

* * * * * * * * * *

Only the Thesaurus imposes a limit on the variations which can be tried on restating the problem. These are generative challenges put within reasonably narrow solvable frameworks.

If the area of search were more extensive and the

boundaries ill-defined, then single key-word searching might be tried.

5.7 Single Key-word Searching

A good example of key-word searching can be found in the lead-in to decimalisation. An interesting discovery was made about the special implication of decimalised money for Wills and Bequests. It derived from the single key-word "Will", and the realization that earlier Wills which specifically mentioned predecimalised amounts of money might be challenged. Changes in the Law were set in motion to keep existing Wills legal.

5.8 Self-interrogation Key-words

At the height of his literary fame, Rudyard Kipling was asked to describe his methods. He disarmingly replied that in no small measure these were a reliance upon six serving men, whose names were Who and Where, What and How, Why and When. This was probably a technique of self-interrogation, established early in his writing development and linked with other creative systems.

Putting aside his actual pronouns, this method of choice probably involved the manoeuvring of successive imaginative questions in which selected fictional characters were examined for motive, setting, age etc. and a variety of narrative threads were then attached to them. Out of this grew scripts formed into stories or novels.

What has been described is the half-aware and highly sophisticated technique of a genius, but it is quite feasible for lesser men to make use of Kipling's "serving men" to produce work enormously improved on what one might have generated without them. This is a semi-intuitive, yet still restricted, economical way of key-word searching. There is, however, another much less imaginative strategy, almost smacking of desperation which can be termed "Happenstance-searching". If the problem can be stated but seems impossible to solve then "Happenstance" can be tried. It can be done with the help of the Shorter Oxford Dictionary as follows:

Find the word at the top left hand column of the tenth page and write it down. It does not matter what part of speech it is (conjunctions are often as useful as adjectives), the significance is that it is a word.

Wait a short while for any association with the problem to emerge. Then repeat the process with the Dictionary, ten pages on, and so on. Such searching can take a long time but it can yield in the long run otherwise impossibly-concealed ideas.

5.9 Memory-lapse

A somewhat different problem, that of slips of memory, can also be caused, as has already been pointed out, by stress and is as annoying as one's loss of creative powers. And this can also be embarrassing to others. We take memory for granted, of course, unmindful that it is a great gift, providing us with our sense of identity and continuity. In this section memory loss caused as a result of stress is discussed.

The case history which follows (p. 98 - 99, Fig. 5.2) illustrates this. Here the lapses are the nagging or unexpected kind, rather than the dramatic or disabling, which are typical of memory-systems disturbed by emotions. For many centuries man has known that emotion interferes with recall, sometimes selectively, sometimes with a general impact. Psychologists still have no accurate, working knowledge of the mechanisms. Often, however, there is an implied meaning to memory-lapse; it seems to operate as a clumsy defence, an attempt to balance-up conflicting attitudes.

The case history indicating many key areas of "forgetting" has been accumulated by a teacher, and it would be beneficial to read through it before embarking on any self-management course, such as Jack (cameo 7) drew up. It is a superb example of the range and scope of manageable memory-lapse not attributable to some serious neurological disease.

Case History

Memory Lapses	Method of Mitigation
1. Inability to recognize which side of the road I should be on whilst driving (only occurs when there is no other traffic around to give "contextual clues").	I make a conscious effort to remind myself which side OF THE CAR should be next to the kerb, before I start any journey.
Frequently now, on entering an empty road, I know I should be "on the left", but I don't know which side is the left.	I've learnt to associate my wedding ring with the side I should be on ... but 'am sometimes given pause by (my right hand) signet ring!
2. Associated with this is an increasing inability to discern the difference between left and right in other situations, 'It's in the left hand cupboard'. I don't know which one that is.	I think I'm worse after a migraine - so allow for it then. I haven't found a way to cope with this yet - if I'm with someone I trust I can ask them to point.
3. Also associated - I don't know which hand to use to open doors. For instance, the O.R.B. telephone kiosk always fazes me!	It only happens because I'm unprepared. If I can prepare myself (as when receiving or giving directions), then I'm O.K.
4. I now forget spellings I once knew well. Recently I wanted to type the word "anxiety", but simply could not recall how it is spelt.	My main strategy is to stop worrying - and leave gaps! (Or spell phonetically, making a note to myself of the need to edit later.)
I wrote it phonetically (angziety) until I remembered and edited. I tried to use a dictionary but, because I couldn't spell the word, I couldn't find it.	
It took about 10 minutes to remember.	

Memory Lapse	Method of Mitigation
5. Many years ago, I forgot my name. I wanted to add it to a list for a theatre visit. Reaching the head of queue I had to drop out until I remembered it. The lapse can only have been a few seconds, but long enough to make me embarrassed and leave the queue.	This has never occurred since - I put it down to a one-off aberration caused by stress of being wildly in love with my English tutor! I do consciously 'retrieve my identity' when I wake from a deep sleep. It's usually there, safely in my head, if I have woken slowly.
6. Last Christmas I invited my parents. (This is a regular feature of our family Christmas.) I am normally 'super efficient' at such organizational/ logistical activities - but this year I realized at 10.30 a.m. on Christmas Day that I had forgotten to buy them presents!	I am usually efficient at such things as entertaining. I have a book in which I keep a record of what was given to whom, and what they gave to us! And a list of people to whom we send cards, and another book in which I record who came to dinner, what I gave them to eat. I don't know how I missed the presents this time.
7. Frequent and increasing lapses occur in my memory for common nouns and adverbs. Ten years ago, after a brain-scan, I was diagnosed as having only 'minimal aphasia'.	a) I tell people (students, for instance). b) I find synonyms -or point - 'please could you pass me that' (for the salt) etc. c) I refuse to worry.

Fig. 5.2 Case History

This case history prompts several important questions, for example,

a) How near is this teacher to the margin of non-management?   and

b) What is the cause of such lapses?

Question (a) ought to be of considerable interest to all lapse of memory sufferers.

Clearly, the subject is a well-organized, and substantially confident woman, who has developed an effective personal system of memory-coping strategies. She has long since appraised the extent of the problem as it impinged on her current role and activities. How much would her coping strategies continue to be effective if either her role became more memory-demanding, or the lapses intensified? There is strong evidence in the history that she has deep reserves of insight and would be capable of developing a greater degree of memory management if either of those two eventualities emerged. It is probable, also, that she would control future role-complexities and would not allow herself to become over-extended. She would, on occasion, also know about, or take steps to discover, more sophisticated mnemonic or cueing systems, deeper relaxation methods, and applications of relaxation techniques to specific, lapse situations.

As to question (b), since she is not an alcoholic nor ageing, the cause must be emotional. Role-stress is clearly indicated which may well have been fueled by long-term, achievement/aspiration conflicts.

Some of the typical issues her memory lapses raise are:

1) Laterality Lapses;

2) Name Forgetting.

1) Laterality Lapses

In the case history the subject tries several methods of laterality-cueing. If there is a general lesson to be learned for all types of memory lapses in this, it is that of anticipation. The teacher in this case does have great powers of anticipation, the ability to recognize stress-sensitive contexts and to have performed the necessary precautionary exercises. She is a determined "lister", generating lists of specific items she may be forgetting.

But then she omits some vital item from the list!

This is a very familiar feature of memory failure. It is a kind of overload which can occur both in the case of deliberately constructed fresh lists and in routine circumstances where no formal lists have been drawn up but the memorizer is relying on habit to gather together all the items which have to be covered.

2) Name Forgetting

There are usually no warnings of any kind before an embarrassing memory-lapse of this kind. Sometimes we can glean an insight into the possible style of forgetting, one of which is influenced by the emotions or deception attached to our relationship with the person named. For example, we may claim unjustifiable acquaintance with a person but be unable to produce the name when challenged.

The context may also be adding its own stress: we may be telephoning, introducing or trying to sell something. Before we telephone or if we are awaiting a call, we can note the key names on a handy card. We can adopt useful evasive techniques for introductions such as Christian names only, with useful tit-bits of biography to head off further enquiry.

5.10 Strategies for Memory Maintenance

Because our human memories are so vast, and so often

reliable, we tend to stray into overloading the system unwittingly.

To help to avoid such occurrences, never bother to remember anything unessential, i.e. being able to retrieve it from a data store, for example, telephone numbers.

Losing the thread, lapses in concentration, can be catastrophic when occuring before a class.

This breakage must not be allowed to cause panic, and one of the most important panic-reducing cues to apply is the instantaneous awareness of the "subjectivity of time". Time appears to pass swiftly or slowly according to the degree of anxiety engendered by the context, and the amount of attention paid by others.

Thus, when we lose the thread and are anxious, an enormous amount of time seems to result before we pick up again. This can be contrasted with the cinema situation, when significant amounts of real time, judged by the clock, slip by in what, when we check subjectively, were seconds only.

That cinema memory could appear to be a useful re-assurance-cue to have in reserve, when "thread-losing" strikes. Thus:

If you lose your thread, adopt the following strategy:

1)   before you try to pick it up, say to yourself:

'I can take my time, it seems just a few seconds, a space to draw breath as far as those listening to me are concerned. I may even be able to use this episode to advantage.'

2)   say out loud: 'Now, where were we?'

3) Ask for questions, and so on.

Techniques to counter memory lapses are many and varied. Below are some examples which may be of use.

a) Cues or prompts, visual or auditory, on cards, tapes, clothes, etc.

b) Lists, simple and complex. Complex especially when narrative is used to cue a sequence of tasks, each step in story being associated with a different task.

c) Jingles and rhymes; initials or words as cues.

d) Special associations for faces and names.

e) Repetition and over-learning to convert material into automatic recall or rote.

f) Special exercises to improve weak recognition skills.

g) Diaries, photo albums and scrapbooks.

h) Relaxation exercises.

The three broad groupings described in chapter 1, the Physiological, Emotional and Cognitive items, upon which Stress can have such an impact, have been discussed through example, and remedies have been suggested to avoid or combat teacher stress through self management techniques.

In the next chapter of this book we shall be concerned with

group management activities in the form of workshops as opposed to self management, although some could be adapted for self management if desired. In the final chapter the workshop brings together all the facets discussed in the book. Both chapters contain useful examples in the form of Figures which groups can copy or adapt for their own use.

6 THE STAFF SUPPORT GROUP AND WORKSHOPS

6.1 Introduction

Where previous chapters have dealt with self management techniques, this chapter outlines a range of tasks, mostly in workshop form, which a staff support group might launch, using the techniques suggested in the preceding chapters. To begin the process, it lays down guidelines for the formation and running of such support group workshops.

Let us not make the error of under-estimating the ingenuity of the individual, confronted with a crisis of stress. However, let us also acknowledge that such crises often summon up the need to act with others, to achieve personal betterment via the route of group solidarity.

Are there any absolute guidelines to indicate the necessity of collective rather than individual action? Actually no, but three points suggest the need for group support for many people:

security, reinforcement and creativity.

When in pursuit of organizational change, the individual remains enormously vulnerable. These are uncertain times and at such times people tend to seek security.

Reinforcement is also an aspect of unity. There is a strong probability that some members of a group will be capable of acting in a reinforcing role. This gives a group power and impetus and differentiates it from the individual acting on his or her own.

Creativity occurs when a combination of several minds comes up with varied solutions to problems. A group can set up a range of ideas, put together a sensible strategy and perform much more efficiently than any group member might alone.

6.2 Setting up a Staff Support Group (SSG)

Put up a notice on the staffroom notice board inviting confidential suggestions as to the need for such a group.

Another method of starting could be to circulate a paper "Questions about Groups". Pressure from teaching unions for group provision within a local authority, or even conversion or adaptation of existing school groups would be another way.

From whichever direction it comes into existence, there are certain responsibilities. On the next few pages there is an example of a "Manifesto for a Staff Support Group". This is only to be used as a guideline, because a manifesto should be agreed informally and collectively by all concerned and should have the concept of shared and rotational leadership.

6.3 Manifesto for a Staff Support Group

1. The Staff Support Group (SSG) shall not be perceived as an "in group", one of the subsidiary duties of every member being the task of presenting the group as an open entity.

2. The SSG should strive for an optimum, effective size, limiting itself by hiving-off if necessary.

3. The SSG should spring out of human necessity and address itself to the satisfaction of needs.

4. The SSG membership, though recruited out of its own different needs, should be representative also of the needs of staff non-members.

5. The SSG activities should be planned and have purpose.

6. Every effort should be made to facilitate the free-expression of individual need, with no judgement on any side.

7. Neither age or sex should be an obstacle to SSG membership.

8. The SSG shall possess outreach facilities and be prepared to admit to discussion staff family members, representatives of parents etc.

9. No member of staff shall be excluded on the grounds of disruptive potential; such difficulties should be regarded as an inescapable challenge.

10. An SSG should be regarded as independent of management.

11. Members of an SSG shall be aware of the necessity to combine complementary strengths and skills for mutual betterment.

12. No member of staff shall consider the stress of group membership worse than the condition which membership is designed to assist.

13. All group members shall share all experiences according to their expressed need.

14. The SSG should exploit its capabilities by a close

collaboration of group members.

15. The SSG should establish a corporate leadership with a rotation, clearly reflecting the changing composition and needs of staff both inside and outside the group.

16. The SSG should encourage men and women with ideas to contribute from outside if they are unwilling to join.

17. The SSG shall reflect a unified profession, regardless of teacher/lecturer union rivalries.

18. Confidential records of the activities and projected programmes should be kept by a designated member.

19. No reasonable supportive technique or idea shall be excluded from the programme of a support group, except those which make unreasonable financial demands on members or are in themselves inducive of stress.

20. The SSG shall not be the sole supportive agency in a school/college, so that official recognition of stress problems is not diminished.

21. SSGs must obtain independent funds to sustain their role.

22. SSGs should be on a district or authority basis, thus enabling powerful shared facilities to be developed.

The following questions should be raised before embarking on the formation of a Group:

a) What steps would you take to raise the levels of institutional, social and individual stress-awareness amongst staff?

b)   How would you establish your own counselling credibility?

c)   What would be your selection methodology for stress-support groups?

d)   Would you cater for staff members requesting individual help?

e)   Would you make operational distinctions between stress generated inside and outside the school/college setting?

f)   What would be your rationale, if any, for forming specialist groups, for example,

1) a job-enrichment group

2) a skills group (focussing on, say, skill deficits such as classroom control, time management)

3) a management group (where the working structure of the school/college might be analysed)

4) a morale group (where depression/burn-out were concentrated upon).

5) a tension state group (where anxiety was the focal point, or memory deficits etc.)

6) a compulsion group.

g)   What would be your policy on school/college home links?

h)   Would you consider it necessary to maintain group continuity during vacations?

i)   How would you evaluate your effectiveness?

Every member has to be aware of his or her responsibilities; the following guidelines should serve to identify these.

1.   Never make a critical comment about another group member without a) some show of regard and warmth, b) some positive suggestion.

2.   Never recount a group discussion to any outside party, no matter how intimate.

3.   Try to introduce at least one positive idea or activity etc. whenever the group meets.

4.   Recognize that every group member has a skill and seek to encourage it, and that every group member has a need and seek to meet it.

5.   Put group suggestions first.

6.   Recognize that, within a short space of time, luck, personal resources, adaptable learning skills etc. may put some members at a greater advantage than others. If you are among the fortunate, remember the responsibility of leadership is the promotion of all group members' welfare.

7.   Be prepared to negotiate etc. on behalf of the group in its needs, finance, equipment, meeting place, and so on.

8.   Realize that leadership is a function of relevant

and current involvement, that it may change and can and should be shared.

9. Recognize that one is fallible and know that others are too.

10. Do not expect to find enjoyment in every opportunity as if it were a pre-ordained reward, nor lead others to expect it.

Every member, too, needs a reminder of the vital observation skill possessed by all. This should be deployed to help the group. We can never be privy to the innermost thoughts of another person undergoing stress. We can, however, try to understand, and our tools of understanding are Observation and Recall.

It is the first of these that notes how the once patient colleague becomes impatient, or the friendly, antagonistic; how effectiveness falls away and motivation weakens. It is the second, our recall of what was, that gives us that insight, our measure of change. Physical change is also apparent, but unlike changes through physical illness they are slow to disappear. We see too that the once careful smoker is transformed into an habitual inhaler and the social drinker, the connoisseur of wine, is verging on the alcoholic ...

* * * * * * * * *

WORKSHOPS. 1) Relaxation   2) Pleasure

Workshop 1   Relaxation

One of the major factors in overcoming stress is the art of relaxation. The first workshop will be concerned with training in relaxation, and following that, the second workshop will concentrate on Pleasure, the overall objective being to show your group how to combine the experiences freely to form a single element in a new lifestyle.

Relaxation is undoubtedly an excellent way of neutralizing or at least minimizing tension. It involves a progressive loosening of muscles, softening of posture and slowing of pace, and can be performed easily in group-relaxation sessions.

As soon as the group assembles, issue the "Guidelines for a Group Member" as shown on pages 110-111, and launch a point-by-point discussion. When basic agreement has been reached, then the Group can be said to be formally founded and work can begin.

The group approach to relaxation is a complex and demanding exercise. Inevitably, such a workshop brings suggestions of physical exercise, prayer meetings and other institutional functions. These undertones must be defused.

There is also the factor that the tempo of each individual's relaxation may not be easily reconcilable with that of the group as a whole.

When we try to assess the balance between relaxation and tension, on a daily basis, we confront two sets of variables and problems of Time and Duration.

Put succinctly, how do we assess the value of formal and informal relaxation experiences, and balance them against the effects of tension?

Framework for Beginning

Fig. 6.1 "Individual Approach Card", Fig. 6.2a "Relaxation Tension", Fig. 6.2b "Ratio" and Fig. 6.3 "Chart and the Assessment", pages 114 to 117, should be copied and given to each member to study.

All members should choose and purchase relaxation aids (music, or pictures), practise all the suggested types of relaxation at home and complete the Assessment card.

Group members should notify the leader when they have settled upon a useful relaxation routine so that a series of developed sessions can be arranged with the group as a whole. (See the chapter 3 on relaxation routines).

First, the Relaxation Assessment Records may be discussed, and a review made of the various methods of relaxation tried.

Whatever may be the convenient length of the sessions, the dominant aspect should be in the form of a formal relaxation period for the whole group. It is an opportunity to put one's chosen relaxation technique under scrutiny and to take the results of such a session to the discussion group afterwards. Observing others relax is also an excellent modelling reinforcement, as is the mildly competitive nature of the event.

The discussion session which may follow could take the previous relaxation experiences as a starting point. With the wide range of relaxation techniques adopted in the group, and the resulting experience gained, individual difficulties and blockings should be rapidly and efficiently solved.

This discussion may need a modicum of structuring and a useful order of topics might be:

A. The effectiveness of the previous, formal, relaxation session - individual reports - creative suggestions, demonstrations and serviceable references.

B.   Pair-working of pictures, slides and tapes if they are losing effectiveness.

C.   The success of formal and informal relaxation during the intervals between meetings. Here the concentration should be upon informal rather than formal opportunities (since most formal aspects will have been covered previously in A), so that discussions generating creative suggestions with anecdotes are valuable. The relaxation/tension ratio records of individual members may now be discussed, plus daily records, and new strategies devised to increase the effectiveness of individual efforts.

At this point, if time allows, a short break for refreshments and a moderate dispersal of members should follow. Dispersal is useful, since unbroken intimacy of the Workshop can be self-defeating. A second, short sequence of formal relaxation in order to pick up and implement the insights gained should follow and before the meeting breaks up, arrangements for the next meeting should be made.

a.	Relaxation notes
b.	Relaxation routines
c.	Relaxation music
d.	Pictures
e.	Relaxation/Tension chart
f.	Opportunities for daily, informal relaxation

Fig. 6.1 Study Card for Individual Approach to Relaxation Developed Sessions

Complete each day:

1)	In Travel (car even)	
2)	In work	
3)	In Toilet/ Rest Room etc.	
4)	At Meal times, Lunch break etc.	
5)	In Work	
6)	In Toilet/ Rest Room etc.	
7)	In Travel	
8)	In the Evening	
9)	Weekend opportunities	

Fig. 6.2a Chart of Opportunities for Formal/Informal Daily Relaxation

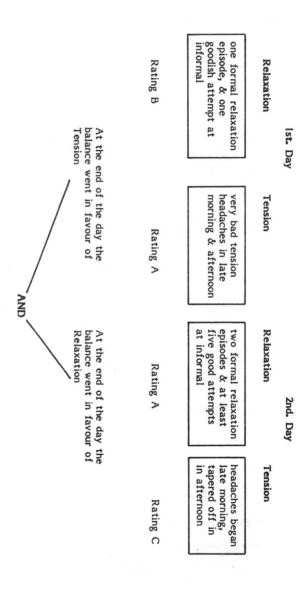

	1st. Day		2nd. Day	
	Relaxation	Tension	Relaxation	Tension
	one formal relaxation episode, & one goodish attempt at informal	very bad tension headaches in late morning & afternoon	two formal relaxation episodes & at least five good attempts at informal	headaches began late morning, tapered off in afternoon
	Rating B	Rating A	Rating A	Rating C

At the end of the day the balance went in favour of Tension

AND

At the end of the day the balance went in favour of Relaxation

already (even after two days) it begins to look as though the tension needs to be combatted by a considerable and successful mix of relaxation to push the ratio into a favourable imbalance. Fresh evidence may soon confirm this early impression.

Fig. 6.2b Ratio

Tick or complete as necessary:

1. My chosen (assigned method of relaxation was

    Type ....

2. I reached deep relaxation in .... minutes

3. How did this compare with previous trials of other types?

    State comparison. ....

4. On a second trial of Type ....

    I noted the following variations:

    a)   Faster time to reach relaxation
    b)   Deeper level

5. On a third trial of Type ....

    I noted the following possibilities of better adaptation.

    (I varied the assigned routine slightly to suit myself)
    Thus (Note adaptations) ....

6. I rate the adaptability of this type of relaxation: A, B, or C.
    (A, most adaptable) in respect of informal relaxation in everyday life.

Fig. 6.3 Relaxation Assessment

Workshop 2 Pleasure

Introduction and Notes

This workshop will deal with ordinary pleasures, suggesting ways of developing these. As with relaxation, so with the understanding of the use of pleasurable moments or activities, stress can be diminished or obliterated from your way of life. More than ever before, the simple, and not-so-simple, pleasures of this life are being trimmed back by pressures of stress, limits of time, fashion or convention.

Man's total experience is set within the boundaries of time, and time's dimension forms one of the vital aspects of pleasure realization. Among the most important of time's contributions are:

a) the extension of time

b) anticipation of pleasure

c) balance of time, periods of stress balanced by periods of pleasure

d) appreciation of time past.

The significant processes involved in a pleasure-deepening programme are, in order of importance, anticipation, realisation and recollection. Recollection is usually the weakest factor, but anticipation is strong and the planning that goes with it pleasurable. Physical pleasures can be divided into three broad categories.

The first group has a definite sensual theme, body-pleasure, capable of being anticipated, realised and recollected, for example, eating and drinking. Two important aspects of food-pleasure are selective regressional eating and the development of a sophisticated palate. We mean by the former a deliberate return to the delights of childhood flavours and dishes. Sometimes we avoid a food because we judge it to be childish. Developing a sophisticated palate can be a continuous source of pleasure by tuning our palates to recognize the finer gradations of taste.

The second comprises physical activities, for example, the state induced by deliberate physical fatigue, as opposed to physical and mental exhaustion, followed by the relaxing bath.

The third group involves care, entailing physical fitness, clothes planning, for example, wearing the appropriate dress for the weather, securely muffled up against the cold or well-ventilated for the heat. Nobody can derive fully the benefits from this Workshop without understanding that pleasure and pain are not necessarily polar opposites, but can sometimes combine to give an increased sum of sensation. We may, for example, go walking in the cold and rain, but, being fit, well-wrapped up and in congenial company, despite a sore heel, enjoy and recollect the day more warmly than many a comfortable, tranquil event.

Not all opportunities for pleasure are immediately obvious: a film may have an off-putting title; the book may have an unappealing cover. These are objective blockings to pleasure, but there are also the subjective blockings, caused by blockings or prejudice in ourselves.

"Pleasures shared are pleasures doubled" is certainly true.

The spectacle of someone else's enjoyment may act as a reinforcer for our own, for it demonstrates that a certain event or experience can undeniably be enjoyed. The feeling of companionship, too, may release additional sources of enjoyment and energy. Pleasures shared with reliable companions are pleasures enhanced and as a self-management routine all pleasures should thus be tested for their social potential.

Framework for Beginning

This workshop has two distinct parts, Introduction and Implementation, the contents of which however will tend to telescope as the Workshop progresses.

The Introduction phase is set out in 7 parts. (See below) Copies of the various figures set out on pages 121-122 should be copied and distributed to members. Several sessions (possibly three) and intervals of a fortnight left between each session will be needed to carry out this stage of the Workshop.

To save time, instruments, tests and case histories can be completed or studied outside the group meetings and results or recollections brought to the Group meeting later.

Introduction

1.   Discussion of Notes on Pleasure (see pp.118-119).

2.   Completion of the Satisfactions Survey (fig. 6.4 page 121).

3.   Introduction and completion by members of the Affirmation/Prescription test for Pleasure (fig. 6.5 page 122) and discussion of the Prescription implications.

4.   The Pleasures Recollection Instrument (fig. 6.6 page 125).

5.   The Pleasure Recollection, Case Histories (pages 123-124). These to be discussed and additional personal Pleasure Recollection Case Histories to be generated by participants and also discussed.

6.   Pleasure Planning case histories to be generated by members and discussed by the group.

7.   The Pleasure/Suffering Ratio (fig. 6.7) to be discussed and members begin keeping a daily P/S ratio.

Tick if satisfied with:

My acceptance by colleagues at work [ ]
My career progress by contrast
    with my abilities   [ ]
The work demands made upon me   [ ]
The purpose and ethics of my work   [ ]

My capacity to take decisions   [ ]
My verbal fluency   [ ]
The relevance and power of my
    established skills   [ ]
My nonverbal flexibility   [ ]
My short-term memory   [ ]
My long-term memory   [ ]
My capability for fresh learning   [ ]
My creativity and originality   [ ]

My present range of interests   [ ]
My capacity to orchestrate
    my interests   [ ]
The relevance of my current
    interests to future needs   [ ]

My sensitivity to beauty   [ ]
My appreciation of harmony in
    music/art   [ ]
My feeling for my surroundings   [ ]
My care for the present
    environment   [ ]
My concern for the future of
    the environment   [ ]

The immediate prospects of my life   [ ]
The longer-term prospects for myself [ ]

Fig. 6.4   Satisfactions Survey

Tick or complete as it applies to you:

1. I can occasionally spot an opportunity for pleasure, but then my depression/anxiety blankets it out.

   ....

2. I can remember I once took pleasure in

   ....

3. I would like to please myself more, in every sense but the brutally selfish

   ....

4. I do not want to experience pleasure or enjoyment

   ....

5. I find difficulty in identifying possibilities for pleasure

   ....

6. There are so many opportunities for pleasure that I am "spoiled for choice".

   ....

Fig. 6.5 Affirmation/Prescription Test

Examples of Pleasure Recollection Case Histories

Amanda

Just thinking about the holiday made Amanda feel good inside. It had been so perfect; the journey had run without a hitch, all the connections had been made; she and her friend had been met by the courier off the airport bus; the sun had come out and shone throughout their stay. She leafed through the colour snapshots that recalled the island trips, the beach cafe, the hike in the mountains and the cheerful vendor of ice cream.

Such a beautiful holiday might not be completely repeatable, but she could certainly try to make sure that something as enjoyable happened again. She determined to look up Tina, an old College of Education friend and suggest that they went to Sweden this time, if she were agreeable.

* * * * * * * * *

Mike

In his tense and miserable state, Mike could recall very little of his past. Some memories however stood out, albeit vaguely. There was the fishing, for instance. He could remember as a teenager that he had gone to the canal with a pack of sandwiches and a vacuum flask and spent the Saturday afternoons float-watching.

And then there had been politics in his twenties. At one point he had been asked to stand as a councillor (the youngest in the municipal elections) but the illness of his father had prevented this. He could recall all those hectic ward-meetings, where issues of great local significance had been discussed.

He'd also had a powerful passion for music then. The big names had been Shostakovitch and Prokofiev, and he had travelled miles to listen to this new confident sound.

Realizing these, he had to struggle to remember accurately all the various parts to the pleasure, so clouded and distorted were they by the unhappiness of the present. However, Martin, who taught craft, had expressed an enthusiasm for fishing. Mike determined to sound him out.

* * * * * * * * *

Meryl

The prospect of a concert was something that Meryl was not going to pass up, but, if she were to extract the maximum pleasure from it, she knew she would have to do some preliminary work.

The advertised programme contained several pieces by a composer new to her, so she borrowed a representative set of his recorded works from the record section of the library, taking care not to cover the programme itself. By this means she hoped to be able not only to catch the freshness of the composer, but also to attune herself to his style.

She read a little of his life-history and began to see how he fitted into the political and social climate of his era.

On the day of the concert she kept a level mood and booked herself a late supper with a friend after the concert was over.

Enter recollections, as age allows, in appropriate column. There is full flexibility in wording possible.

Long Term	Short Term
I took pleasure in: (10 years ago)	I took pleasure in: (1 year ago)
....	....
....	....
....	....
(20 years ago)	(18 months ago)
....	....
....	....
....	....
(30 years ago)	(2 years ago)
....	....
....	....
....	....

Questions: How do Long Term and Short Term pleasures compare?

Can you rank your pleasures?

Fig.6.6 The Pleasures Recollection Instrument

When we try to assess the balance between pleasure and suffering on a daily basis, as was mentioned earlier we confront two sets of variables, the problems of time and duration; that is, how do we assess the value of pleasure episodes and balance these against the experiences of suffering? We do this by charting our daily pleasures and severity of suffering, both on an A. B. C. D. E, rating. A = maximum pleasure and maximum suffering.

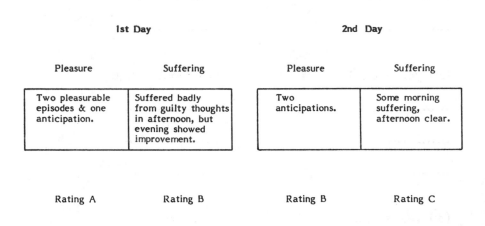

1st Day		2nd Day	
Pleasure	Suffering	Pleasure	Suffering
Two pleasurable episodes & one anticipation.	Suffered badly from guilty thoughts in afternoon, but evening showed improvement.	Two anticipations.	Some morning suffering, afternoon clear.
Rating A	Rating B	Rating B	Rating C

Already there seems to be an acceptable holding ratio between pleasure and suffering with pleasure the dominant factor. Fresh pleasure-seeking will probably make that ratio even more favourable.

Fig. 6.7 Pleasure/Suffering Ratio

Finally now that we have discussed and analysed various techniques for overcoming stress we can try to put into practice all that has been discovered in these chapters by tackling the final workshop described in the next chapter, Renewing Motivation (Individual and Group Motivation). This combines interest-deepening and job-enrichment, and both are highly structured in the section which follows.

Notes

7 MOTIVATION AND STRESS

7.1 Introduction

This final chapter describes a workshop, which encompasses everything discussed and practised in the previous chapters. It is aimed at renewing your motivation for work in school and college. The workshop tackles this problem, focussing upon the needs of teachers to renew that motivation which has been lost in the coils of stress.

To begin the process it is suggested that the Staff Support Group sets up an Interest-Deepening sub-group to work on the initial programme of this workshop. Having studied the other workshops, and using them as a guide to embody previous insights and hints, the group could launch the programme as a practical exercise.

The concepts of "interest-deepening" and "job-enrichment" have to be combined if the renewing of motivation is to succeed completely.

First, however, the Interest-Deepening sub-Group must be set up to begin the whole process.

7.2 An Interest-Deepening Group (IDG)

This sub-group needs first a working manifesto or mission statement which should be studied, discussed and agreed in principle by all potential members of the sub-group. It can serve as a selection device; only those members who are prepared for the onerous task of renewing motivation should be involved.

1. The Group sustains anticipation-training for members.

2. An IDG is an interest in itself.

3. Its exclusive aim is interest-development and re-motivation.

4. Members keep Interest-Deepening Diaries, the entries in which are available to the group.

5. Its dominant concern is problems, not feelings.

6. It should contain a mix of members, both those comfortable and those uncomfortable in their teaching roles.

7. It should be prepared to perform as a brain-storming group.

8. It needs to meet regularly.

9. It should consist ideally of eight to ten staff members.

10. It should be prepared to represent its members' interests to management, especially concerning job-enrichment.

It is necessary to get a base-line and a pattern of dissatisfaction from every sub-group member. The "My Work" questionnaire (Fig. 7.1) on page 131 is designed to fulfil this need. Every member should be asked to complete it, putting

'Yes' or 'No' at the end of each statement.

I wake without enthusiasm for my work.   ....

I wake with a decisive revulsion
for my work.   ....

My lack of enthusiasm is persistent.   ....

My lack of enthusiasm is intermittent.   ....

I fantasise a job-change, occasionally.   ....

I fantasise a job-change, often.   ....

I am positively negotiating to change
my job.   ....

I view my work as pointless.   ....

I view my work as sabotaged by lack of
management interest.   ....

I view my work as impossibly difficult,
given current circumstances.   ....

I view my work as emotionally
unrewarding.   ....

I view my work as financially
unrewarding.   ....

I believe my earlier job-satisfaction
could be salvaged.   ....

I believe I am suffering emotionally/
physically because of lack of
job-satisfaction.   ....

Fig. 7.1 "My Work"

Having completed this questionnaire, they should then be given a second set of statements, to be answered in the same way, on "My Teaching Life" (Fig. 7.2) shown below, which should uncover deeper, more distant dissatisfactions.

1. I have been consistently challenged and worsted by favouritism during my working life.   ....

2. I have frequently found myself in rivalry situations.   ....

3. Much of my work has been exploited.   ....

4. I have been significantly blocked by authority.   ....

5. I have found declining interest has gone hand in hand with diminishing creativity.   ....

6. My energy has gradually decreased.   ....

7. A substantial part of my effort has been abortive.   ....

8. Often there was a deceptive, initial success attached to my projects.   ....

9. My work sometimes put me in humiliating, inter-personal situations.   ....

10. I seemed to drop into a loser-pattern midway in my career.   ....

11. I discovered signs of increasing work stress, not compensated by job-satisfaction, during my career.   ....

12. I became more 'out of touch' with the underlying philosophy of my work, as time went by.   ....

Fig. 7.2. My Teaching Life

Several discussion sessions should be allowed for the two sets of findings.

Then the Workshop can move on to an in-depth analysis of personal interest from a lifestyle history perspective.

Using Figs. 7.3 (page 134) and 7.4 (page 135) every group member can analyse the past in detail. The analyses open up, first, the general teaching-interest account, and second, the detailed history of past anticipations.

When each set of results is presented to the whole group, members should be able to grasp the renewal opportunities which are revealed.

At the same time they could take into account the following questions, what can be called "Time and Interest" in relation to Motivation:

1.   Is there a potential sustainer in the traditional cyclical rhythms of teaching?

2.   Is the passage of time and unavoidable repetition a potential destroyer of interest?

3.   Is the structured, process-dominated timetable for teaching, an interest-depleter?

4.   Does the passage of time and inevitable experience of change give grounds for presupposing the emergence of renewed interest?

5.   What is the role of urgency in the maintenance of interest?

Where was the interest once?	State the **previous** signific- ance of factor 1-5 (1=max)	State the **current** value of factor 1-5 (1=max) value.	Explain the reason for the current valuation.	Explain the reason why betterment would be difficult
Was it in the experience of technical competence?				
Was it in the anticipation of greater technical mastery?				
Was it in the immediacy of results?				
Was it in the certainty of future results?				
Was it in the evident appreciation of pupils?				
Was it in the positive response of supervisors?				
Was it in the friendship of colleagues?				
Was it in prestige which surrounded the work?				
Was it in the interest displayed by family members?				
Was it in the financial rewards of the work?				
Was it in the security of work?				
Was it in the appreciation of being in work?				

Fig. 7.3 Interest Recovery Instrument
(Where was the interest once?)

Expectations?	Outcomes?	Benefits?	Credits?	Lessons?
The items of anticipation	The way events turned out	The positive spin-offs & results	The person-al credit that you desired	What lessons may be learned

"The use of recriminating about the past is to generate workable strategies for the future."

Winston Churchill

"The past is another country."

L. P. Hartley

Fig. 7.4 Expectations, Outcomes, Benefits, Credits, Lessons, (can be used as Diary Model)

Group members should then start to keep an "Interest-Deepening" Diary using the framework of "Expectations, Outcomes, Benefits, Credits, Lessons (EOBCL) (see Fig. 7.4 page 135).

The purpose of this diary will be to chart and reinforce growing work interest. The following questions can be discussed by the IDG as a help in reinforcing interest.

a)   Could a member teach a developed, external interest, and thus enhance in-house work satisfaction?

b)   Could a member discover or re-capture the original thrill by meditation, focussed-imagery or twilight technique (all discussed in previous chapters)?

c)   Could a member try "re-labelling"? For example, "threat" converts to "challenge", "risk" to "opportunity".

d)   Could a member try anticipation technique, for example, deliberate programming of future pleasurable events?

e)   Could a member use a searching system to explore fresh angles of interest in routine practice, for example, micro- and team teaching; computer-aided instruction/learning; interactive video/audio and so on?

f)   Could a member select those aspects of teaching which give pleasure in enlargement or reinforcement?

7.3 Job-Enrichment

Interest recovery or deepening can often be helped by a programme on job-enrichment. The Staff Support Group could enlist their sub-group in launching a "Job-Enrichment Study" to suggest the feasibility and desirability of job-enrichment, identifying staff-admitted needs and their ideas for it, and as a result create a climate for job-enrichment.

In order to clarify group ideas the Staff Support Group should start a discussion using the following questionnaire as a basis:

Does the teaching profession need job-enrichment theory or practice?

What do teachers understand by the term job-enrichment?

What are the possible parallels in teaching with industrial/commercial job-enrichment techniques, for example, team-working; self-evaluation; responsibility-developing etc.?

Is there a stage of disillusionment/burnout in teaching where job-enrichment might be useless?

To what extent does job-enrichment in teaching depend upon cognitive restructuring?

To what extent does job-enrichment in teaching depend upon the implementation of techniques such as relaxation?

To what extent does job enrichment in teaching depend on uncontrollable factors like salaries, social esteem etc.?

If job-enrichment requisites vary from teacher to teacher, are there any commonly-agreed necessities?

Does teaching present a unique sort of challenge to a would-be job enricher?

Might teaching be unique in that it could only be enriched by off-the-job activities?

Is the role of the educational administrator decisive in job-enrichment for teachers?

Is there any special quality appertaining to a profession which renders job-enrichment superfluous?

Do the differing contexts of teaching, Infant, Primary, Secondary, Further, Higher, Continuing etc, present special challenges?

This questionnaire poses many difficult questions; the notes which follow may help to answer them.

Notes

First and foremost the question should be asked whether your present job is worth enriching. Given that the task of enhancing the value of any job is a daunting one, might it not be better to seek other work which will supply the satisfaction now lacking. Unfortunately this immediately gives rise to a trio of associated questions:

What are the chances of securing a new job?

What is the certainty of finding job-satisfaction in such a job?

What might the price be, for example, re-training, re-location, reduction in earnings etc. etc.?

Only when all these questions have been answered honestly in the negative, can the challenges of job-enrichment be met. It is a challenge. There are two sets of essential, though not exclusive, job-enrichment propositions: A and B.

A. Investing the job with greater personal meaning,

for example, developing:

Broad-range feedback for staff (results awareness)

Greater staff involvement in broader tasks

Staff counselling, for example, a) affording staff members the chance to alter their subjective frame of reference, thus allowing relabelling of tasks for the benefit of morale, b) developing interest-intrication of tasks, whereby staff can discover fresh aspects of the work to encourage re-motivation.

B. Elimination or modification of causes of job-stress and frustration.

These tend to be organizational or managerially-influenced. There is, for example, work-stress tied into noise, heat, light, cold, smell, access, facilities.

The impact of the work itself in terms of training, deployment etc. is important. Is the work too demanding, frightening, fatiguing, uninteresting?

Or are there specific stress-related issues associated with the work. For instance:

a) Tempo (incompatibility, too slow, too fast)
b) Standards (management/employee differences)
c) Rivalry (promoted etc)
d) Discrimination
e) Harassment
f) Uncertainty (direction, official supervision)

7.4 Diagnosing and Prescribing

These lists are outlines to be filled in by means of creative staff discussion. It is possible to plan and implement several useful job-enrichment schemes on your own account, depending on your own inner resources, but the greatest majority of job-enrichment changes are brought about by the action and pressure of Staff Support Groups.

The activities of individuals in the initiation and sustaining of such Staff Support Groups (SSGs) are vital.

An individual can be the catalyst which begins the process whereby the SSG is formed. It can also be the individual's role to generate an appropriate needs analysis, using, for example, the suggestions and implication of the propositions A and B above. The individual can search for information on various aspects of enrichment, the key words being work-stress, burnout. The individual may be motivated by the group to negotiate with management the vital enrichment changes.

Change is required for job-enrichment, and when perceived as challenge, stress is reduced and enrichment guaranteed. When members finish such creative discussions, which are akin to brain-storming sessions, they may be aware of more questions than answers and remain in a debating rather than implementing stance.

Two tasks may profitably be introduced at this stage:

1) implementing concepts

2) action/adjustment.

To form the basis of the task, Fig. 7.5 page 141 suggests adaptations of a traditional range of job-enrichment implementing concepts A - H .

Action/adjustment shown in Fig. 7.6 on pages 142-3 shows a list of educational items capable of being tested and analysed in terms of the concepts already mentioned. The aim is to discuss the feasibility of these items in the light of the concepts, selecting and grouping the items, and, if possible, supplementing them.

Implementing Concept		Definition	Adaptation
A.	Natural units of work =	ways of distributing work to fit natural rhythms	Enlightened timetabling?
B.	Principles of Ownership =	guaranteeing privacy and space	Work-space focus?
C.	Client-Relationships =	establishing positive contact with those who use the service/ product etc.	Counselling pupils/ students, human-relationship, curriculum all-through-school-contact?
D.	Task-Combination =	attack on over-specialization.	Broader teaching responsibilities? Broader personal responsibilities?
E.	Vertical loading =	higher responsib-ilities, brought downwards.	Disciplinary and practical role delegated?
F.	Task-Feedback =	information on task-performance	Pupil/parental feedback to teacher?
G.	Task Advancement =	increasing responsib-ility levels.	Special respons-ibility schemes research, PR etc?
H.	Environmental Optimising =	improving the work environment.	Redecorating and landscaping school/college

Suggested adaptations of a traditional range of job-enrichment "implementing concepts"

Fig. 7.5 Implementing Concepts

Note that two concepts H and B are omitted from that analysis.

Because of the important environmental issue it raises concept H will be found in a special addendum in Fig. 7.7, page 144. This provides another exercise for the group, giving an opportunity for them to consider wider than professional enrichment concerns.

Concept B, by common consent the most significant of the eight, is left until last.

"Notes on Teaching and Personal Space " on page 145, can be used to form the basis of a group exercise on the concept. Such an exercise presupposes creative solutions. For example, a response to personal-space concerns may be to partition classrooms; a feasibility study of such a proposal can be introduced, and arguments for and against it noted on a sheet as in Fig. 7.8 on page 146.

(N.B. These items are only roughly grouped and not defined in detail. They are to be used as a guide or basis for discussion)

Sensitive personal issues
Pecking order mysteries
Promotion (true)
Promotion (inverted, power without status)
Demotion
Recognition (in school)
Recognition (out of school)

Better match of personal rhythms to:
Timetabling
Term lengths
Continuity
Team-teaching
Home-school liaison
Subject-shift
Subject amalgamation
Subject separation

More aids
Fewer aids
Independent evaluation of performance
Local, in-school, evaluation of performance
Training, in-service etc.
Micro-teaching evaluation & training
Research on school-catchment attitudes
School centred research,
Curriculum methods

Post-pupil research on:
Opinion, opinion-change,
Direct use of instruction
Indirect use of instruction

Staff-organised events
Staff seminars
Staff exhibitions
Staff projects with parents & children
Departmental staff meetings
Inter-departmental staff meetings
Staff encounter groups
Staff relaxation
Staff outings
Staff appearance

Financial & Economic Considerations
DIY
School-based economies
Bulk buying
School perks

Fitness for Work
In-school fitness sessions
School environmental health

Subjective techniques
Brain-storming
Cognitive restructuring
Auto-desentisization
Re-motivation techniques

Fig 7.6 Suggested Action/Adjustment Items

Direct

e.g. targeted enrichment to provide exclusive betterment for teaching staff.

Indirect

e.g. global enrichment of school/college environment, benefitting all, students & staff.

Built/adapted

example:

Pigeon-hole frame for teacher/ lecturer mail and messages

Privileged System

example:

Numbered parking spaces for staff cars

Built/adapted

example:

Noise reduction via carpets and absorption materials.

Other suggestions

Fig. 7.7 Job-Enrichment - Special Addendum for H

"Teaching and Personal Space"

What do we mean by personal space? There are probably three aspects, represented by concentric circular areas (see diagram below). The innermost area is intimate space where social distance (person to person) or privacy (activity/ possessions) are preferred. The hatched area of the diagram is that domain which the individual indisputably controls. The dotted area is the sector of wider influence which the individual shares with others.

Although the concept is not easily reconciled with the role of teaching, we might identify the first with the teacher's person, desk or locker; the second with his or her class or lecture room; and the third with the department.

The first can be called Intimate Space, the second, Environmental Domain, and the third, Sphere of Influence. The balance of all three seems important to the maintenance of teachers' morale, and job-enrichment can be linked with them.

The framework shown in Fig. 7.9 page 147 sets out the three and in the course of the feasibility study each member of the group can complete it in terms of Description, Drawbacks, Recommendations and Assessment.

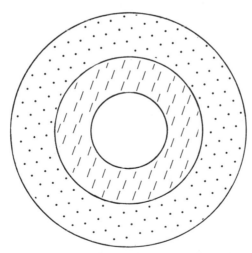

Personal Space

Personal Space

The proposal is for all classrooms, with sufficient window-space, to be one-eighth/one quarter partitioned to a height of seven feet. The cubicle thus formed will have a sliding door, desk-flap, cupboard and independent lighting. A communication system might be installed, linking office to cubicle. The purpose is to give the classroom teacher a private space, for study, storage, communication etc.

Arguments for	Arguments against

Fig. 7.8 Feasibility study on arguments for and against inner-partitioning of classrooms

Component	Your Dissatisfactions	Your Recommendations	Your assessment
Intimate Space Your own description of existing specification.			
Environmental Domain Your own description of existing specification.			
Sphere of Influence Your own description of existing specification.			

Fig. 7.9 Framework

In Conclusion

Crises of Stress often summon up a need to act with others. These last chapters have suggested a range of activities which Staff Support Groups might set up in the form of workshops, together with helpful worksheets in the form of figures which can be copied and handed to members. It is hoped that these workshops will be used to help those in the teaching world to overcome the causes and symptoms of Stress and give them a whole new outlook on their professional life.

Notes

Bibliography

Beck, Aaron, T. (1972) *Depression, Causes and Treatment.* Pennsylvania, USA: University of Pennsylvania.

Cooper, Cary, Cooper, R.D, Eaker, L.H. (1988) *Living with Stress.* Harmondsworth: Penguin.

Dryden, W. and Gordon, J. (1988) *Thinking Your Way to Happiness.* London: Sheldon Press.

Juniper, Dean F. (1989) *Successful Problem Solving.* London: W. Foulsham & Co.

Juniper, Dean F. (1976) *Human Relationships for Schools and Colleges* (A teacher's manual for organising a human relationships programme). London: Centre for Stress Management.

Reddy, M. (1987) *The Manager's Guide to Counselling at Work.* London: Methuen.

Suinn, Richard (1990) *Anxiety Management Training and Behaviour Therapy.* London: Plenum Publishing Co.

Materials available from the Centre for Stress Management, London.

Video - "Stress, how it can be controlled and managed".

Audio-cassettes on relaxation, mediation, smoking-reduction, depression.

INDEX

Index cont.